# SERVICES FOR OCCASIONS OF
# PASTORAL CARE

# SERVICES FOR OCCASIONS OF PASTORAL CARE

## The Worship of God

### Supplemental Liturgical Resource 6

*Prepared by*

The Ministry Unit on Theology and Worship
*for the*
Presbyterian Church (U.S.A.)
*and the*
Cumberland Presbyterian Church

*Published by*
Westminster/John Knox Press
Louisville, Kentucky

For acknowledgments, see pages 137–138.

Published by Westminster/John Knox Press
Louisville, Kentucky

PRINTED IN THE UNITED STATES OF AMERICA
2  4  6  8  9  7  5  3  1

**Library of Congress Cataloging-in-Publication Data**

Presbyterian Church (U.S.A.)
    Services for occasions of pastoral care / prepared by the Ministry Unit on Theology and Worship for the Presbyterian Church (U.S.A.) and the Cumberland Presbyterian Church.
        p.    cm. — (Supplemental liturgical resource ; 6)
    Includes bibliographical references.
    ISBN 0-664-25153-6
    1. Presbyterian Church (U.S.A.)—Liturgy—Texts. 2. Cumberland Presbyterian Church—Liturgy—Texts. 3. Presbyterian Church—United States—Liturgy—Texts. 4. Occasional services—Texts. 5. Church work with the sick. 6. Spiritual healing. 7. Forgiveness of sin. 8. Baptism—Reaffirmation of covenant—Presbyterian Church. 9. Church work with the terminally ill—Presbyterian Church. I. Presbyterian Church (U.S.A.). Ministry Unit on Theology and Worship. II. Cumberland Presbyterian Church. III. Title. IV. Series: Presbyterian Church (U.S.A.). Supplemental liturgical resource ; 6.
BX8969.5P74 1990                                                    90-36452
264'.051370982—dc20

# CONTENTS

# PREFACE

God is love. We know that this is true when we contemplate what Jesus has done for us. God gave Jesus Christ to be the life of the world. Jesus came into the world, the author of John's first letter affirms, "so that we might live through him." The author continues: "Beloved, if God so loved us, we also ought to love one another" (1 John 4:9–11).

The source and motivation of pastoral care is the love of God. When the church in the exercise of this ministry calls on the Holy Spirit to draw near—

> Come, of comforters the best, . . .
> What is wounded, work its cure[1]

—it witnesses to Jesus, the Good Shepherd. Jesus, the first pastor among all, bids us cast our anxieties on him, for he cares about us (1 Peter 5:7).

This book is prepared for the use of all who are engaged in any ministry of care, whether ordained or lay. "Pastoral Care," as the term is used here, includes the ministry of compassion extended by elders and deacons and other members of the community of faith as well as the caring ministry of a pastor. This is in keeping with the broad definition in the Directory for Worship:

> Pastoral care is the support which Christians offer one another in daily living and at times of need and crisis in personal and communal life.[2]

This volume, *Services for Occasions of Pastoral Care*, is the sixth in the series of Supplemental Liturgical Resources. This series has its origin in actions taken in 1980 by the churches that formed the present Presbyterian Church (U.S.A.) and by the Cumberland Presbyterian Church. These churches acted to begin the process of developing "a new book of services for corporate worship" and expressed the hope that the new book would be "an instrument for the renewal of the church at its life-giving center." The process called for a series of volumes for trial use before the finalization of the book of services. The Supplemental Liturgical Resources series is the response to that action.

The Administrative Committee of the former Office of Worship of the Presbyterian Church (U.S.A.) appointed a task force in 1986 to prepare a resource for ministry with the sick and the dying. The progress of the task force was monitored by the Administrative Committee through 1987, and since then it has been monitored by the Theology and Worship Ministry Unit of the Presbyterian Church (U.S.A.). Those who served on the task force were Thomas D. Campbell; Jung Han; William P. Lytle; Ross Mackenzie; Thomas Mainor; and Neddy Mason (chairperson). Dennis J. Hughes and Kenneth L. Vaux served as consultants.

In 1989, the work of the task force was extensively tested and many evaluations and suggestions for its revision were received. The manuscript was carefully revised in response to the testing and was subsequently approved for publication by the Theology and Worship Ministry Unit.

This resource seeks to draw together the three reference points necessary for pastoral ministry in a Reformed understanding: biblical theology, the worship of God, and the life of the people of God in the particular church.

*Services for Occasions of Pastoral Care* is therefore presented to help pastors and visitors in their ministry with the sick and the dying, in the confidence that it will provide the kind of help in pastoral care that other volumes in the series have provided for other aspects of the worship of the people of God.

Those who served on the Administrative Committee of the Office of Worship that appointed the task force and monitored its early work were Melva W. Costen; Helen Hamilton; Collier S. Harvey, Jr.; Robert H. Kempes; Wynn McGregor; Ray A. Meester; Robert D. Miller; David C. Partington (chairperson); Robert Stigall; and Harold M. Daniels, Director of the Office of Worship, and Marion L. Liebert, Administrative Associate of the Office of Worship.

Those who served on the Theology and Worship Ministry Unit committee monitoring the completion of the work of the task force were Ruben P. Armendariz; José H. Bibiloni; Sandra Hanna Charles; Harland Collins; Melva W. Costen; Donna Frey DeCou; Margery Curtiss; Joseph G. Dempsey; Burnette W. Dowler; Gershon B. Fiawoo; Richard Fiete (current chairperson); Daniell C. Hamby; Roberta Hestenes; Thomas L. Jones; Clements E. Lamberth, Jr.; Daniel W. Martin; Raquel Montalvo; Deborah Mullen (former chairperson); Peter Ota; Douglas Ottati; Heath K. Rada; Marilee M. Scroggs; James C. Spalding; R. David Steele; Benjamin M. Weir; Mary Jane Winter; and staff of the worship function of the Theology and Worship Ministry Unit: Harold M. Daniels; Nalini Jayasuriya; and Janet Wolfe. Those serving on the Worship Sub-Unit as the task force work was being reviewed were Ruben P. Armendariz; Melva W. Costen; Donna Frey DeCou; Daniell C. Hamby (chairperson); Robert T. Henderson; Daniel W. Martin; May Murakami Nakagawa; Donald W. Stake; R. David Steele; and Mary Jane Winter (past chairperson). The counsel of George B. Telford, Director of the Theology and Worship Ministry Unit, and of Joseph D. Small, Associate Director, as well as of other members of the Unit's staff, has provided valuable guidance. The care given to details by Cindy Ohlmann Stairs, worship administrative assistant, and Regina J. Noel, worship secretary, and accuracy in manuscript preparation were aspects in facilitating the meeting of deadlines, completing the testing, and achieving a smooth moving from the work of the task force actions to the completed book.

We invite your evaluation of this resource presented to the church for trial use as it anticipates a new book of services. Send your comments to the Theology and Worship Ministry Unit, Room 3408, 100 Witherspoon St., Louisville, KY 40202-1396.

HAROLD M. DANIELS
Associate for Liturgical Resources
Theology and Worship Ministry Unit

# INTRODUCTION TO SERVICES FOR OCCASIONS OF PASTORAL CARE

# I
# A HISTORY OF PASTORAL CARE

In all religions the care of the sick and the dying is both an obligation and an expression of loving compassion. According to the rites and forms of each religious tradition, the recurring crises of broken relationships, alienation, grief, forgiveness, sickness, and death have called forth various forms of pastoral care. In Judaism, as early as the first three chapters of Genesis the central issues of pastoral care are evident: God's creativity and help; human potential and brokenness; family alienation and the promise of reconciliation; and the persistence of hope even in the face of despair and death.

## Pastoral Images: From the Hebrew Prophets to the Ministry of Jesus

The mission of the prophet in early Israel was not only to declare the divine message to various groups among the people but also to show pastoral vigilance in seeing that the will of Yahweh was put into effect. The prophets of the classical period directed their message to Israel in general but left it to each individual to make the appropriate application. Ezekiel, an heir to this tradition, enlarged this pattern not only by announcing God's judgment to the individual but also by developing what we can legitimately speak of as a "cure of souls." (See Ezek. 18:30–32, and compare 33:10. Even though God will punish the guilty, repentance may still save those who persist in a life of righteousness.) The priesthood was involved in dealing with the sick only in certain cases where the disease entailed isolation from the community by some ritual defilement.

In his own ministry Jesus continued the prophetic tradition of proclaiming God's will for the people and for the individual. He also fulfilled and transformed such terms as Son of man, prophet, and especially servant. His whole life was a ministry of service. He came not to be served but to serve (Mark 10:45). His disciples do what he has commanded: to love one another (John 15:12). The primary Christian vocation has therefore always been (in Carl Jung's phrase) to "wander with a human heart through the world."

The Christian ministry of pastoral care derives not only its warrant and energy from the risen Jesus but also its inspiration and imagery. Jesus is the Good Shepherd (John 10:11). The background of this Gospel description in the Hebrew scriptures is the messianic idea of shepherding God's people. God is the Shepherd of Israel (Ps. 23:1; 80:1; Isa. 40:11). The term was also applied to God's anointed rulers such as David (Ps. 78:70–72). The new thought introduced by Jesus is that the Good Shepherd gives his life for the sheep. Pastoral ministry in the church of Jesus looks to this example and finds its inspiration in the vigilance, courage, and loving compassion of the Good Shepherd.

## Pastoral Care in the Early Church

*Ministry Grounded on Baptism*

What Jesus began, the disciples continue. Empowered by his Spirit, they appropriate and hand on his ministry. As he taught, so they teach; as he was baptized, so they enter into his baptism and baptize those whom he has called; as he was raised from the dead, so they too walk in newness of life:

> We have been buried with him by baptism into death, so that, just as Christ was raised from the dead by the glory of the Father, so we too might walk in newness of life. Romans 6:4

In contrast to the baptism of John the Baptist, which was a baptism of water "for repentance" (Matt. 3:11), the baptism of Jesus is for death and resurrection. The baptism of Jesus is a sign, or sacrament, of passing over from a death like his so that we may be united with him in a resurrection like his (Rom. 6:5).

Baptism is thus the constitutive event by which we are made disciples and members of Christ's body. It is the center and source of the church's life and ministry. Every ministry of the church derives its meaning and validation from the sacrament of baptism. Baptism is the ordination of the Christian to the continuing ministry of Jesus Christ.

*Continuing the Ministry of Jesus*

The baptismal narrative in each of the Synoptic Gospels (Matt. 3:13–17; Mark 1:9–11; Luke 3:21–22) is followed by a clear sequence: first, the wilderness experience (Matt. 4:1–11; Mark 1:12–13; Luke 4:1–13); and then, the first preaching of the reign of God (Matt. 4:17; Mark 1:14–15; Luke 4:14–15, and especially 4:16–30). We can assume that during the wilderness experience Jesus pondered his distinctive call to the ministry of the reign of God. Thus the sequence in each of the Synoptics is baptism, call to ministry, and preaching the good news of God's reign.

This pattern is universal in early Christian documents that deal with baptism. A church order of the third century, for example, the *Apostolic Tradition* of Hippolytus, elaborates on the simpler New Testament texts but preserves the same sequence. Candidates for baptism are taught the essentials of the faith in preparation for a lifelong discipleship. In the initiatory rite they are first anointed with the oil of exorcism. The anointing, with its renunciation of attachment to the world, is reminiscent of John's baptism of repentance. They are then baptized in the name of the triune God. A second anointing follows with the oil of thanksgiving, or blessing. This anointing is a sign of the indwelling of the Holy Spirit with its grace and blessing. Finally, the newly baptized participate in the baptismal eucharist and receive communion for the first time. With the full baptism act complete, they are now ready for service to Jesus Christ and to the world: "Each person must hasten to do good works, please God, and live a good life." They are sent, as Jesus himself was sent, with good news for the poor and the sick.

Those who carried the gospel of Christ into the Roman Empire shared alike in one thing: they were baptized and they had responded to Christ's call to ministry. Not even its critics could deny them an achievement of compassion unequaled in the Roman world: the pastoral care of the sick, dying, bereaved, poor, and troubled in every Christian community throughout the Roman Empire. Such love (*agapē* is the Greek word) comes to expression within the Christian community in the manifold forms of pastoral care.

Paul refers to this *agapē* in a famous text (1 Corinthians 13). The text follows immediately after his list of the gifts of the Spirit to the church, among which are healing and the ability to help others

(1 Cor. 12:28). The second reference to healing (v. 30) as a gift suggests that dealing with the sick—whether by way of comfort, treatment, or cure we do not know—was a ministry of special importance among the first Christians.

The well-known text in James 5:14–16 indicates that cases of illness were a special concern to the church. Intercession for the sick, here called "the prayer of faith," implies a trusting expectancy that the power of the risen Christ was still available to heal. Healing, however, was not simply a physical cure, and the reference to forgiveness (James 5:15–16) implies that the elders could authoritatively declare the forgiveness of God, as Jesus himself had done (Mark 2:10; etc.). The passage clearly implies a pastoral care or cure of souls involving visitation to the sick person, spiritual conversation, confession and absolution, and physical recovery.

*Sickness as a Sphere of the Divine Activity*

Early Christian theology characterizes sickness and death as signs of the brokenness of God's good creation. Creation had lost its intended wholeness, or *shalom*. In contrast, healings and health were a restoration of God's intention.

Two pastoral consequences flow from this sense of sickness as the sphere of the divine activity. First, sickness, distress, and pain can paradoxically be the occasion in which we may discern the work of the healing, suffering, dying, and risen Savior. Indeed, so far from seeking to avoid the pains of the world, we may receive them as the sphere where, in the midst of death, Christ is at work giving life to the world. Thus, Augustine writes:

> When all goes well with you, when the world smiles on you, no one in your family has died, no drought, hail, or fruitlessness has attacked your vineyard, your wine-cask is not sour, your cattle haven't failed, you have not been shamed in any high worldly position, your friends all survive and think well of you, your dependents want nothing, your children obey, your slaves tremble before you, your wife is harmonious with you and the house is happy—then find tribulation, if in any way you can, that having found tribulation, you may call on the name of the Lord.[3]

## Pastoral Care Before the Reformation

By the end of the eleventh century, Catholic Christianity was dominant in the life of Europe. Pastoral ministry centered on the power of divine grace to heal afflictions of body, mind, and spirit. The Fourth Lateran Council (1215) enjoined priests to "pour wine and oil into the wounds of the one injured after the manner of a skilful physician" (Canon 21). On the assumption that bodily disease is sometimes caused by sin, the council decreed that "when physicians of the body are called to the bedside of the sick, before all else they admonish them to call for the physician of souls, so that after spiritual health has been restored to them, the application of bodily medicine may be of greater benefit" (Canon 22).[4]

The medieval church taught that seven sacraments—baptism, confirmation, eucharist, penance, extreme unction, ordination, and matrimony—had all been instituted by Christ, though not all were necessary for salvation. All were capable, however, of applying the merits of Christ to the believer.

The sacrament of penance secured the forgiveness of actual sins committed after baptism. Confession allowed the priest, serving as a physician of souls, to probe and inquire into the spiritual and moral life of the penitent. A distinction was drawn between sins for which the sacrament was necessary—mortal sins, serious sins committed in full knowledge and by free will—and those sins which could be forgiven without the sacrament—venial sins, sins committed with less full knowledge or in a lighter matter. Confession became a transaction involving the individual confessor and the penitent and not the whole congregation. The procedure for examining the conscience and for guiding the penitent was psychologically searching. Yet although the intention was a sensitive concern to free individuals from the burden of sin, in practice the effect was often to reduce Christian living to correct ethical behavior.

Protestants have frequently criticized the medieval pastoral tradition for its formalism. No doubt abuses existed, but confession and the visitation of the sick contributed to the physical, social, and spiritual wholeness of the Catholic community. Penance provided a pastoral and sacramental means of interaction between the pastor and the penitent. It allowed the penitent to lay down a burden of conscience that was painful or troublesome. The visitation of the sick brought the minister of Christ into the homes of the people, and prayers for the sick assured them that nothing separated them either from the love of Christ or from the affections of the body of Christ.

### The Cure of Souls in the Reformed Family of Churches

All the reformers rejected the medieval sacrament of penance and insisted on the necessity only of unmediated confession to God by the penitent sinner. On the other hand, all recognized the value of confession in the public assembly for worship and in private confession to a trusted counselor. The counselor would ordinarily be a minister of the Word, but any lay person might exercise this ministry.

In his year of marvels, 1520, Martin Luther (1483–1546) published a treatise on themes of pastoral care—the seven aspects of evil and the seven complementary blessings of God. He intended the "Fourteen Comforts for the Weary and Heavy Laden" to help scrupulous and burdened souls to find their way to a gracious God. All assaults on the human soul, including plague, disease, and sickness, yield to the victory that Jesus has won in his suffering, death, and resurrection. Such assaults drive the sick and the dying to participate in the grace of God. Christians should therefore take the opportunity to serve others in distress as an opportunity to minister to Christ: "If we meditate on these joys of the power of Christ and on these gifts of his grace," Luther said, "how can any small evil distress us?"

The pastoral ministry of the Reformed churches that followed Luther took shape first in Switzerland and Scotland.

### Zwingli and Bullinger

In 1518, Ulrich Zwingli (1484–1531) was called to become the people's priest at the cathedral, or Great Minster, in Zurich. Within five years he brought the city council to approve his new program for reform. Faithful preaching of the gospel, he said, must be followed by faithful pastoral care. Christ's whole work of redemption would be of no avail if sinners were not made whole thereby. Since the old disciplines had broken down—and particularly the sacrament of penance—new methods must be devised. In the matter of confession, private confession to God is more than adequate, but if it would help, the penitent may seek out a wise counselor, a minister of the Word.

Zwingli's son-in-law and successor, Heinrich Bullinger (d. 1575), stands out as a model of the Reformed pastor. He advanced the preaching and pastoral ministry begun by Zwingli. With patience and tact he visited refugees, the sick, and the dying. The Second Helvetic Confession (adopted in 1566), which has always enjoyed high regard among the Reformed churches, was in a sense Bullinger's last will and testament. In regard to confession, it follows Zwingli.

Auricular confession (a priest's hearing an individual's confession) is not forbidden, although anyone overcome by sin and temptation may take counsel of a minister "or any other . . . learned in the law of God."[5] In regard to pastoral ministry, the duties of a minister include comforting the fainthearted, rebuking offenders, raising the fallen, providing for the poor, and visiting the sick. The sick have a special call on the pastor, who is to pray with them and for them, and to see that as they die they "pass happily from this world."[6]

## John Calvin and John Knox

John Calvin (1509–1564) advanced the work begun by Zwingli and shifted the center of gravity of the Swiss reformation from Zurich to Geneva. Like Zwingli, he insisted that the pastoral office has a double function—preaching and the encouragement of a life of holiness: "The office of a true and faithful minister is not only publicly to teach the people over whom he is ordained pastor, but as far as may be, to admonish, exhort, rebuke and console each one in particular." In the Sunday prayer of intercessions Calvin provided this prayer for any in affliction of body or spirit:

> O God of all comfort, we commend unto thee all those whom thou dost visit and chasten with cross and tribulation, whether by poverty, prison, sickness, or banishment, or any other misery of the body or affliction of the spirit. Enable them to perceive and understand thy fatherly affection which doth chasten them unto their correction, that they may turn unto thee with their whole heart, and having turned, receive full consolation and deliverance from every ill.[7]

Calvin's undeserved reputation as the stern lawgiver of Geneva has hidden the wise and gentle side of his pastoral ministry. Many of his letters deal with the predicament of death. His own wife, Idelette, died in one of the city's plagues. For Calvin, the acceptance of death is a testimony to the grace that reconciles us to God. In death we may become all that God has called us to be—obedient in this as in all of our life to the God in whom we both live and die; for "whether we live or whether we die, we are the Lord's" (Rom. 14:8).

In one of his letters Calvin describes the death of a friend, Mme. de Normandie, who in dying confided in him her trust in a loving God. We may note two points in the description. First, members of the church are present with the dying and share in the ministry to the dying. Second, the dying woman remembers words from the church's Sunday worship which she rehearses for her comfort.

While she was thus discoursing, a considerable number of persons came in. I threw in from time to time some words, such as seemed suitable; and we also made supplication to God, as the exigency of her need required. After once more declaring the sense she had of her sins, to ask the pardon of them from God, and the certainty which she entertained of her salvation, putting her sole confidence in Jesus, and having her whole trust in him,—without being invited by anyone to do so, she began to pronounce the *Miserere* [Ps. 51] as we sing it in church, and continued with a loud and strong voice, not without great difficulty, but she entreated that we would allow her to continue. Whereupon, I made her a short recapitulation of the whole argument of the psalm, seeing the pleasure she took in it. Afterwards, taking me by the hand, she said to me, "How happy I am, and how I am beholden to God, for having brought me here to die."[8]

In Scotland, John Knox's instructions for the visitation of the sick provided the model for all subsequent pastoral ministry in the Reformed churches:

Because the visitation of the sick is a thing very necessary, and yet, notwithstanding, it is hard to prescribe all rules appertaining thereunto, we refer it to the discretion of the godly and prudent minister, who, according as he seeth the patient afflicted, either may lift him up with the sweet promises of God's mercy through Christ, if he perceive him much afraid of God's threatenings: or contrariwise, if he be not touched with the feeling of his sins, may beat him down with God's justice. Evermore, like a skilful physician, framing his medicine according as the disease requireth, and if he perceive him to want any necessaries, he not only relieveth him according to his ability, but also provideth by others, that he may be furnished sufficiently. Moreover, the party that is visited may at all times for his comfort, send for the minister: who doth not only make prayers for him there presently, but also, if it so require commendeth him in the public prayers to the congregation.[9]

*Confession and Absolution in the Reformed Tradition*
Calvin treated the old system of repentance and confession much as Luther and Zwingli had done. The old system of auricular confession had burdened consciences and in place of offering comfort produced either despair or hypocrisy. It was, Calvin said, "in so many

ways pernicious to the church." But since confession can also be recommended as an aid to those who need it, he proposed three kinds of confession for the church. In the first, the assembled congregation implores pardon through Christ's ambassador "furnished with the mandate of absolution." In the second, an individual who has been the occasion of offense to the church declares repentance and is restored to the unity of the congregation. In the third, however, Calvin declared that private absolution is efficacious and beneficial when it is used by those who need relief of conscience:

> For it often happens that one who hears general promises that are intended for the whole congregation of believers remains nonetheless in some doubt, and as if he had not yet attained forgiveness, still has a troubled mind. Likewise, if he lays open his heart's secret to his pastor, and from his pastor hears that message of the gospel specially directed to himself, "Your sins are forgiven, take heart" [Matt. 9:2 para.], he will be reassured in mind and be set free from the anxiety that formerly tormented him.[10]

The minister as Christ's ambassador confirms and seals the grace of the gospel in the mind of the penitent.

In Scotland, the Book of Discipline, largely the work of John Knox (1515?–1572), set out a procedure for dealing with offenses that moves from a private warning to admonition, then to public rebuke, and finally to a solemn—and terrifying—excommunication. Only when the offender was determinedly unrepentant was the name made known to the congregation. The congregation was to determine whether sufficient sign of repentance had been afforded; if so, then the offender was to be led to make public confession and be restored into full communion. Otherwise the offender was to be excommunicated. None but the family were to communicate with the offender, unless it seemed to the church authorities that such contact might produce a conversion.

Knox's Liturgy (1560) gives elaborate instructions concerning "offenses that deserve public repentance." The intent was not to encourage any gloating over others' sins but to express publicly the authentic biblical insight that if one member suffers, all suffer together, and that there should be no discord in the body (1 Cor. 12:25–26). Public confession was therefore good for the health of the congregation and an opportunity for the penitent to be "received again into the society of Jesus Christ."

No time need be spent in tracing the decline in public and private confession within the Reformed family of churches. The scheme had degenerated into a pious legalism by the eighteenth century. The congregation ceased to be a welcoming society of Jesus Christ. For a symbol of the degeneration of the scheme we may refer to the kirk session minutes of St. Cuthbert's parish church in Edinburgh. A young man adjudged guilty of a sexual offense was condemned to stand in the white sheet of the penitent outside the west door for four consecutive Sundays. Laconically, the session recorded that on three consecutive Sundays "John ―――― compeared," that is, appeared at the west door. The fourth entry states: "John ―――― did not compear: he having gang dementit." John had gone out of his mind. The system had broken a spirit too sensitive for public shame. Little wonder that the confession of sin before representatives of the congregation disappeared. Within a short period even the private assurance of God's grace for the relief of conscience had lost its value in the church's ministry.

In the twentieth century the pastoral care movement is in many ways a ministry of reconciliation. It has become one of the chief means of interaction between counselor-pastor and client-penitent. While no one school or form of pastoral care has the resources to deal adequately with every need of the human heart, and while some forms of pastoral care have lost touch with the distinctive resources available in the Christian faith, the achievements of the pastoral care movement have served the churches well. When it is most effective, pastoral counseling allows the emotionally burdened or overloaded to lay down feelings of guilt or disturbance of conscience otherwise too painful to endure. At its best, contemporary pastoral care restores a Reformed understanding of the dynamics of confession and absolution, as set forth in the Second Helvetic Confession, where the focus is entirely on God's accepting grace:

> Ministers, therefore, rightly and effectually absolve when they preach the gospel of Christ and thereby the remission of sins, which is promised to each one who believes, just as each one is baptized, and when they testify that it pertains to each one peculiarly. (Second Helvetic Confession 5.100)

## Pastoral Care Today

In considering the church's ministry of pastoral care today, we need to be sensitive to what it means to experience sickness, healing, dying, or death in a distinctive modern context. Today we take our illnesses to the physician and go to the hospital to die. Illness tends to be a hidden experience which we try to resolve with medicines, surgery, counseling, or "just bearing it." We interpret sickness as a natural event, a consequence of some fault in our constitution or behavior, or some mechanism gone awry that needs fixing. At the same time, we suffer and die at the mercy of an impressive technology, in institutions shaped by economic and legal values, and in the light of day as a public spectacle.

A recovery of the pastoral elements in both the Catholic and Protestant traditions can help us come to terms with the modern experience of sickness and death. The emphasis of the Roman Catholic pastoral heritage on penance and expiation recognized, despite its excesses, the fact that Christ took on the sins, pain, and death of the world in his passion and thereby purchased release and health for a suffering humanity. This ministry of forgiveness and healing was entrusted to the church. The Protestant pastoral heritage in its emphasis on personal accountability, purity, and uprightness of soul understood the drama of disease and death, health and salvation as a deeply intimate drama of God's working in the individual soul. The Catholic and Protestant traditions of incorporation and participation provide a foundation today for an appropriate interpretation of the plight of sickness and dying and for an attentive pastoral care.

All ministry as the service of love takes its shape around the human needs that it encounters. This is true whatever form that ministry takes: teaching, preaching, initiation into the Christian community, the eucharistic breaking of bread, saying prayers for others, or serving the people of God in any manner. A loving community expresses its care in many different ways.

# II
# A THEOLOGY OF PASTORAL CARE

To be ill, suffer, or die is a universal human experience. The unique aspect of illness, suffering, and death in their modern phases is that they typically occur in a larger context of alienation, dread, and fear of the abyss and loss of the self. Sickness, suffering, and dying are therefore occasions not only for professional care but also for an openness to the meaning of divine grace and the assurance of forgiveness. In other words, sickness and dying are occasions to rehearse our baptism into Christ. Then and with a deepened awareness we can confess (in the well-known words of the Heidelberg Catechism) that Christ is "our only hope in life and death" (Question 1).

A theology of sickness and dying, and an appropriate pastoral care for our time, require that we rightly interpret the religious heritage as well as the modern experience of sickness, healing, and dying. Our spiritual heritage reminds us that the human condition and plight are not a meaningless and mechanistic event but a focal point of divine action in our world and in our personal being. Creation and fall, sin and grace, evil and redemption are theological words we use to interpret this experience of travail and renewal.

Particular aspects of theology distinctive of the Reformed tradition are useful in considering the church's ministry of pastoral care.

## The Priority of Grace

In its definition of salvation, Reformed theology has characteristically treated the doctrine of grace as the article by which the church stands or falls. The question is really one about whether grace or faith has the priority. A theology of grace lays its stress on nurture; a theology of faith lays stress on conversion. For Knox, salvation is by grace, not by faith. Faith does not reach up to grasp grace, as though grace could be achieved by human merit. Grace is not a state or condition to which we may attain, if only we believe enough. For Knox, that would be to turn faith into a human initiative.

This conviction about the priority of grace created among Presbyterians a quite distinctive style of preaching and pastoral ministry. It produced a style of evangelical preaching and a nurturing and evangelical view of the sacraments. The preaching of grace presses upon all the assurance of God's love. The ministry of pastoral care seeks to do no less. As we accept that God speaks the first word—whether in salvation or wholeness—our ministry will witness to God's prevenient grace, and our pastoral care will nurture people so that they may come to rely utterly in life or in death on that surrounding grace. Nowhere do we become more aware of God's nurturing grace than at the Lord's table. Archibald Johnston of Warriston (b. 1611), one of the first Covenanters, speaks of how wonderfully God called him to communion at the age of fifteen: "As many communions, so many comforts."

### Justification and Acceptance

Knox, in his debate with James Tyrie, a Jesuit, argued that the controversy between the Protestants and the "Romanists" was the same as that between Paul and the Judaizers of Galatia, in which the gospel of grace through faith was at stake, "for it concerneth the chief head of justification." In the Reformed understanding this means that Jesus Christ is central for faith and for life. Salvation is exclusively the work of God in Christ. We must look away from ourselves in order to look to Christ alone for salvation. So we must be on guard against putting anything in place of that salvation, whether it be psychological theory or pastoral technique.

This insistence of the reformers remains as important as it was in the sixteenth century. One of the most frequently used calls to worship among the Reformed churches gives expression to this: "Our help is in the name of the LORD, who made heaven and earth" (Ps. 124:8). Justification by Christ alone means rejecting all forms of self-justification and turning to Jesus Christ alone for wholeness. The Reformation insistence on the priority of grace has radical consequences in regard to pastoral care. Jesus Christ has opened a way to

God, so that we can approach God solely through Christ and on the basis of what Christ is and does. The ministry of pastoral care is a means by which the individual comes into a caring and healing relationship with Jesus Christ. Ministers or pastoral caregivers cannot therefore substitute their own personalities or skills for Christ's humanity and healing. Otherwise, a new sacerdotalism will emerge in which the human qualities of Christ are replaced by the human qualities of the pastor. A psychological sacerdotalism is no improvement on a sacramental sacerdotalism.

The pastoral implication of the doctrine of justification is the principle of acceptance. To know what it means to be personally acceptable to Christ is likely to make it easier for a pastor or counselor to accept the person who comes in need. It also makes it easier for such a person to be open to the ministry offered, to accept feelings without fear of moral judgment, and to find release and healing. As in the ministry of Jesus, so the pastor, the counselor, and the caregiver respond from within their own acceptance to Christ. Pastoral care means seeing and seeking the best in the concrete situations of life. The criterion is neither a set of abstract principles nor a system of casuistry but a recognition that each individual has the potential to grow to the fullness of the measure of Christ.

## A Present Savior and the Ministry of Presence

The same themes that we have seen in the ministry of Jesus and the disciples recur in pastoral care. All true ministry is a continuation of the work that Jesus began. His ministry remains the supreme inspiration and example of those who provide some form of pastoral care. This is especially true when we attempt to apply his sufferings and death to the needs of the sick and the dying. The Gospels announce a God who is neither remote from nor indifferent to human weakness and misery. God is implicated in all pain and death, and the resurrection speaks of God's triumph over sin and death.

The words of the angel at the tomb have particular meaning for persons engaged in this ministry: "He has been raised. . . . He is going ahead of you to Galilee" (Mark 16:6–7). The pastor, counselor, or caregiver is not alone in ministry but is in the company of the risen Christ. To visit a house where there is trouble or a hospital where there is sickness is to enter a sphere where Christ is already present. For this reason we are not to see the patient as a passive recipient of care but rather as an active participant in a unique situation in which that person's openness to healing is itself a witness to the present reign of Christ. The patient's very life situation opens up possibilities for us to receive and be grateful for the grace of Christ. We see that grace in the faith, patience, or love of the patient, in the patient's own acceptance of the illness or trouble.

Pastors often wonder about the best way to bring spiritual care to the sick and the dying; so do the friends of those who by reason of illness have been cut off from their familiar surroundings. The ministry of Jesus, the present Savior, comes to expression in the first instance in the simple presence of the pastor, the family member, or the friend.

The pastoral visitor, however, has more to offer than mere presence. To come to those who are sick as a believing Christian is to come with the faith that God's grace can make the broken whole and lift the fallen.

Perhaps nowhere else does a Christian's own appropriation of the faith play so great a part as in ministry to another in distress. Authentic pastoral care is incarnational. It grows out of both the brokenness which is our universal human condition and the wholeness which God is everlastingly renewing by grace. As we acknowledge the reality of our own brokenness and yet experience it as overcome, we bear witness to the grace that neither sickness nor death can resist.

# III
# WORSHIP IN PASTORAL CARE

The prayers and services contained in this resource provide ways in which the church can minister to the needs it encounters through scripture, prayer, and sacrament.

They are aids to the service of God's grace, but only to the extent that they express the faith of the believing community. They cannot be substitutes for a living faith in the healing power of the church's Lord. It is therefore important for caregivers to be conscious of their own woundedness and their own experiences of healing grace. Only then can these prayers and forms be instrumental in bringing one person's interior whole-brokenness and broken-wholeness to meet another's. In their meeting ground will be Christ's healing presence.

## Ministry with the Sick

In sickness and in the process of dying, the body is subjected to invasive procedures from without and painful reactions from within. Disease has its characteristic arrays of smells, disfigurements, and embarrassments. Among the sick and their friends and family members who stand around them we may see fear, anger, worry, helplessness, and frustration. The sick and the dying desire release from *all* that pains them, emotional troubles as well as physical. To this extent they are more often aware than are the well of their need for Jesus Christ to satisfy them in their struggle to cope with the pains of their condition. They look for an assurance that Christ is with them as the one who comforts and makes whole—the high priest who is able to sympathize with our weaknesses (Heb. 4:15). To the extent that the sick and their families find that assurance, we may also see a renewal of trust, companionship, acceptance, and, above all, love.

God is present with the sick. So those who are sick become witnesses to the grace and power of God to help in time of need. Pastoral ministry mediates the care of God for any who are in distress of body, mind, or spirit. God uses human instruments for such ministry: friends and family members, nurses and physicians, pastors, therapists and technical assistants of various kinds, and a variety of visitors. Each in some manner brings care, professional skill, or practical help. Some have a particular responsibility to pray for the sick and to encourage them during their illness. But any pastoral visitor can be a bearer of God's grace.

It is important also to recognize that those who suffer may also be very special bearers of God's grace. Illness can be a vocation, a calling, an occasion for a new ministry. Pain in Christian vocation is therefore not simply an irritant to be anesthetized or drugged away. It is an experience to be fathomed as an occasion of judgment and grace. Pain is an opportunity for something new and holy to happen to us. The sick and the dying not only need to receive pastoral care but may become witnesses and ministers to others by virtue of being recipients of God's action.

## Pastoral Visits

This resource suggests a wide variety of scripture readings that may be used in pastoral visits (pp. 44–46) and provides texts of the readings most frequently used (pp. 47–63). Sentences from scripture (pp. 41–43) may be used as introductions to prayer in visitation or as calls to worship in the services provided in this book. Prayers are provided (pp. 64–70) for use or adaptation in a variety of circumstances. An appropriate scripture sentence may be selected by the visitor to leave the person at the end of the visit. This can give encouragement long after the visit has ended.

## Conversation

Characteristics of good conversation with the sick are sincerity and a communication that involves careful listening and mutual respect. The patient will quickly sense whether the visit is one prompted by duty or by sincere regard and affection. The helpful visitor does not control the conversation but allows the patient to indicate what direction it should take. A patient is in some sense a captive—to the illness, to the bed, to the routine of hospital or nursing home, and even to the well-wishers who come by. It is a caring act to engage the patient as an active subject in the give-and-take of true conversation and not to treat the patient as an "object" to be soothed or informed.

It is not helpful for the visitor to speak in clichés about how God sends suffering as a test. The visitor may say, "I know how you feel," but that is patently untrue. Only the sufferer knows the feel of this suffering. Feigned cheerfulness for the sake of the patient will simply provoke resistance, for it evades what is in the heart and soul of the patient. On the other side, sickness does not necessarily bestow either nobility or gracefulness on disagreeable or selfish persons. A sensitive pastoral visitor, however, can help the egocentric patient to grow in character and the ability to love others.

Difficulties other than illness may present themselves in the conversation. For example, patients sometimes express concern that their stay in the hospital keeps them from attending to daily responsibilities. When members of the congregation learn of these concerns, they are often willing to help the patient by tending to such tasks as caring for pets, providing transportation, and the handling of household finances. A simple gesture such as bringing the church flowers or the bulletin can express the continuing bond between the congregation and the patient. Good words can be spoken that lift the spirit, give joy, or strengthen faith. They may be Bible verses, hymn stanzas, psalms familiar from childhood, or the like. To one, we can say: "I'm here to tell you we miss you and want the best for you." Of another, we can inquire whether any help is desired. But however simple and plain in speech, the visitor also has a word that points to our ultimate hope: "God is our refuge and strength, a very present help in trouble" (Ps. 46:1).

*Scripture-Reading*

In the reading and hearing of scripture we are reminded of the story of God's saving acts, comforted by the promises of God, and renewed by the presence of God. It is good, then, for the pastoral visitor to read a portion of scripture during the visit.

The selection taken from scripture will usually be brief and chosen with reference to the particular circumstances of the patient. Often a passage already familiar to the patient will best provide comfort, encouragement, and reassurance. The suggested readings and texts from scripture given in this resource (pp. 41–63) will be useful.

*Prayer*

One of the most important ministries of care and worship that a pastor can perform is that of praying with the patient, including prayer for the patient by name. Prayer through the Holy Spirit gives voice both to the cries of human pain, need, and hope and to the depths of God's steadfast love and healing grace.

When visiting people who are ill, pastors sometimes hesitate to offer prayer, not wanting to intrude on the patient's privacy or to risk embarrassing a patient who may be uncomfortable with public prayer. It is wise to be attentive to the patient's needs, feelings, and desires regarding prayer. On most occasions the patient desires and welcomes prayer, and it is neglectful to miss the opportunity to pray with and for the person by name. If there is any doubt about the appropriateness of prayer, the visitor can simply ask the patient whether prayer is desired.

A selection of prayers suitable for various situations is provided in this resource (pp. 64–70). These prayers can also suggest language and themes for extemporary prayer when that form of prayer is more suitable.

*Sick Children*

When the patient is a child, any of the psychosocial aspects of adult-child relationships may come into play. In the pastoral visitation of a sick child, at least three groups of adults are involved: the medical personnel, the parent(s) and other adult visitors, and the pastoral visitor. Each has a distinctive relationship to the child.

The value of fairy tales for a child, in the view of many child psychologists, is that they answer the child's implicit question. The question is not one of fact: "Is this true?" It is one of security: "Am I safe? Am I safe in a world of dragons and wicked witches?" The child who is in a hospital will take an interest in the facts of illness according to age and intellectual capacity. But at any age the implicit questions of a patient, and particularly of a child, have to do with security. The illness itself, and even the threat of death, will be alarming to a child only to the extent that parents or visitors convey fear, anxiety, or stress. Whispered secrets about the unknown are likely to be more frightening to a sick child than strange medical equipment, the purpose of which has been simply explained. Discussing in honest simplicity the nature and likely progress of the illness can help also.

Parents and pastoral visitors can both share in appropriate activities with the child—for example, watching television or playing games.

The suitability of prayer in visits to a child is one that common sense and sensitivity will determine. The visitor can repeat a known family prayer and intercede for other sick children in the room or hospital. If a spoken prayer seems out of place, the visitor can say simply, "I'll remember you when I say my prayers tonight."

*Length of Visit*
The patient has less room to maneuver for privacy than the visitor does. The considerate visitor respects the right of the sick person to receive medical attention, or even to go to the bathroom without an outsider present. A way to judge the right length of the visit is to take cues from the patient. After receiving pain medicine, a patient may simply want to hold the visitor's hand and fall asleep. Generally, ten to fifteen minutes suffice, since ill persons tend to weary quickly and may find it embarrassing to ask a visitor to leave.

Extended illness of a chronic rather than acute nature involves a different pattern in visitation. Lengthier visits, for example, are appropriate. In a brief illness, visits may be frequent, but in extended illness there tend to be longer intervals between visits. Even friends can seem to withdraw from the long-term patient. Regular visits over extended periods provide an opportunity for telling family stories, recalling common memories, and enlarging friendship. The very duration of extended illness can provide an opportunity for a patient to develop a pastoral relationship of a depth previously unexperienced.

*Qualities Helpful in Pastoral Visits with the Sick and the Dying*
The same approach that applies to any pastoral visit is no less appropriate in the care of the sick and the dying.

1. *Realism:* Death is the end of a life. It is definite and final. It is no comfort for one on the sickbed to hear words of false hope or a comfort that hides the truth.

2. *Hopefulness:* It is not only for this life that we have faith in Christ, as the apostle teaches (1 Cor. 15:19). God never ceases to love us— that, certainly, is true—so we are all safely lodged with God wherever we are in life or in death.

3. *Truthfulness:* It is neither pastorally helpful nor philosophically possible to give a good answer to every question about suffering and death. The sensitive visitor of the sick or the dying does not need to know why this crisis has occurred, let alone what God is doing. What is necessary is loving presence.

4. *Conviction:* The words of Job interpreted by Handel have conveyed a hopeful message to many in time of trouble: "I know that my Redeemer liveth" (Job 19:25). The occasion of sickness or trouble enables a friend to speak with conviction about the things that abide.

5. *Resourcefulness:* Dying and death are supremely inconvenient. They never come at the right time. People who are inconvenienced appreciate appropriate help. Good help is simple, immediate, and practical. Various people have their own ministry to offer in the hospital room—including the housekeepers. The good visitor allows each to perform the appropriate ministry.

6. *Sensitivity:* Like houseguests, visitors to the sick can often outstay their welcome. The visitor should watch for signs that the sick one is tiring or does not feel up to the visit. The thoughtful visitor does not arrive at a bedside with preconceived ideas of what needs to be done or said. The visitor who regards the visit merely as a routine to be performed will not be able to share in what can be a mutually enriching ministry.

7. *Perceptiveness:* Sickness and death can call forth painful and unpleasant feelings such as anger, bitterness, resentment, and despair. The accepting caregiver does not judge such feelings and will allow the sick person to express them without offering criticism or judgment. When such feelings are heard and accepted, they can change, releasing the person to move toward a better or more comfortable place.

8. *Openness and expectancy:* In each situation the key question is, What is the potential in this situation, and how can it be experienced most fully? How do we appropriate the gift that God is offering in what is immediately before us?

9. *Attentiveness:* Even the busy doctor or nurse can avoid conveying a sense of being too busy or preoccupied; so also the pastoral visitor. Accepting the patient's invitation to be seated communicates that the visitor is eager to give undivided attention. Declining to sit may indicate that the visitor is in a hurry to attend to other important business. It is neither necessary nor helpful to determine in advance the course of the conversation. The considerate visitor listens carefully not only to the words being spoken but also to the feeling behind the words. The patient may say that everything is well but may also convey a quite different message by tone of voice or facial expression.

10. *Listening together to the story of our salvation:* The word "salvation" is closely bound up with the idea of wholeness. The ministry

of the caring pastoral visitor is to set forth in word and deed the gospel of salvation through Jesus Christ. Jesus shared our life, pain, and death. Jesus' death is an event that has transformed all things. Jesus is not unfeeling. We are not alone, ever. Prayer during ministry to the sick and dying can help raise the dying into the dimension of the resurrection. Even the dying can bear witness to the resurrection of Christ, for when the mortal puts on immortality, "then the saying that is written will be fulfilled: Death has been swallowed up in victory" (1 Cor. 15:54).

## Holy Communion for Those Unable to Attend Worship, and Especially the Sick

To receive communion is not only a spiritual comfort but a sign also of the unity of the Christian community. In the Lord's Supper all who love Christ are one—the sick and the well, the living and the dead. Pastoral ministry provides a critical link between the sick person and the congregation. Part of this ministry is to reassure the patients that the congregation is praying for them at worship. In receiving Holy Communion, the ill remember the community from which they are at present separated, and are reconnected in a spiritual manner with that assembly.

Among the Reformed churches the celebration of the Lord's Supper is not a private ceremony but a part of the public worship of the whole people of God. The session may authorize the celebration of the sacrament in connection with the visitation of the sick. On such occasions at least one elder shall be present in addition to the minister. In the Reformed understanding, a sacrament is a seal to the word. The reading of scripture and a brief sermon normally accompany the rite. If they are familiar, the traditional greeting ("Lift up your hearts . . .") and hymn of praise ("Holy, holy . . .") may be said by the persons who are present. The room may require that the celebrant administer communion in a manner suitable to the space and conditions.

The Lord's Supper may be administered to the sick in the manner proposed in this book (pp. 73–80) or with a minimum of ritual and ceremonial. Each mode has its virtues. The more formal will evoke memories of the congregation at worship. In the crisis of illness the repetition of familiar words—the Twenty-third Psalm, for example—brings a sense of stability. The room of the sick, however, may suggest a very simple celebration of the Supper.

The service, whether formal or simple, will include at the least the reading of scripture with a brief interpretation, the words of institution, and a eucharistic prayer. The eucharistic prayer will include a thanksgiving for creation and redemption and an invocation of the Spirit. Different parts of the service can be assigned to the persons who are present.

If a patient is unable to eat or drink, the spiritual communion binding those present includes the patient. A patient who receives nourishment only through intravenous measures is still a communicant in the Supper, even without receiving the bread and the cup, if the desire and the intention are present with the prayer of faith.

### Service for Wholeness

In a variety of ways the church has a commission to minister wholeness: communion with God made whole; community with one's neighbor made whole; and a relationship to the created world itself made whole. A service for wholeness is provided on pages 83–96 for use with congregations. A similar service is also provided for use with an individual (pp. 101–108). The latter service is intended for use in a hospital or a nursing home with individuals who are unable to attend a congregational service of wholeness.

In New Testament times, sickness and death were regarded as signs and consequences of sin. Accordingly, Christ's healing ministry (Matt. 9:35) was a sign of the messianic age as was the healing ministry of the apostles (Matt. 10:1; Luke 9:1; Mark 6:7, 13).

In their ministry to the sick, the community of believers first offer intercession for healing and wholeness. They pray in response to what they have heard in scripture and sermon. Opportunity is given to pray for the specific needs of any who are present. In the laying of hands on the sick, those who take part can see an outward sign of their prayer of faith that God will come in healing grace. Even if the sick are absent, they are still part of the community gathered for worship. This suggests that friends or relatives be encouraged to receive the laying on of hands representatively for the sick for whom they pray. While it is not necessary for any who come forward to make known their request, it is helpful for the minister and elder(s) present to have the information for brief conversation at the time or for pastoral counseling later. Both minister and elder(s) participate in the laying on of hands. As in the visitation of the sick, anointing may also be included in the service as a sign of God's grace and healing mercy.

The anointing of the sick has been part of pastoral ministry from New Testament times (see Mark 6:13; James 5:14–15). It is to be understood in terms of its spiritual effect as an external sign of the presence of Christ, who continues his ministry of salvation and healing. It can add a spiritual strength to the sick person's life by deepening the trust, confidence, and affection of the recipient and give assurance of Jesus' gracious willingness to heal and to forgive sins. It is neither a magical act nor an outmoded ritual. It does not replace medical care, nor is it a means of producing healing, at least in the sense of a cure. Physical healing may indeed follow the anointing, but such healing is always from God and normally through God's agents of healing. Spiritual healing—the lifting up of the spirit to God or a personal appropriation of salvation in Christ—is quite distinct from physical healing or cure.

The oil used in anointing is traditionally the finest grade of olive oil or chrism.[11] Chrism (a mixture of olive oil and aromatic oils) used for anointing is etymologically related to the name Christ, the anointed One or Messiah. Chrismation can be a helpful sign of their life in Christ to any who have recourse to this means of grace. It is appropriate to offer a prayer of thanksgiving for the oil as a gift of God's bounty. A lovely prayer of Hippolytus (ca. A.D. 215) said over the offering of oils has been preserved:

> O God, sanctifier of this oil,
> as you give health
> to those who are anointed
> and receive that with which you anointed
>     kings, priests and prophets,
> so may it give strength to all who taste it,
> and health to all who are anointed with it.[12]

Congregational singing may take place during the laying on of hands. The singing, especially if it is of a prayerful nature, may be the congregation's way of sharing in the prayers. The selections may be from the list of hymns, psalms, and spiritual songs on pages 97–100, or from other sources such as the collections of music from the Taizé Community in France, especially those employing appropriate biblical texts.[13]

## Service of Repentance and Forgiveness

Even persons who have heard God's general promise of mercy in the gospel sometimes remain in doubt concerning the forgiveness of their sins. The sick and the dying, too, may need to be relieved of a burdened conscience. Jesus Christ is the only Savior and our mediator with God. Nevertheless we hear and receive the forgiveness of sins in a variety of ways. It is a powerful assurance for the troubled in spirit to hear a minister of the gospel declare that God is gracious and forgives and welcomes the penitent.

The recovery of a ritual that proclaims the good news of God's grace and forgiveness, such as the one on pages 111–113, is not a denial of the Protestant heritage but a recovery of its core: God graciously accepts the returning sinner. To proclaim the gospel from the pulpit is one thing; to make that gospel personal in confession and the appropriation of God's forgiveness is an act of caring ministry.

The penitent person and the minister may sit face-to-face in the church or in some other place. The traditional sign of forgiveness is either the laying on of hands or the extension of a hand over the penitent, with or without the sign of the cross.

## Reaffirmation of Baptismal Vows for the Sick and the Dying

Our whole life is to be lived with particular reference to our baptism. In baptism we share in Christ's death and resurrection. Baptism is therefore a sign of the wholeness and healing that God promises. Baptism is so central to our discipleship, it gives meaning in every circumstance of life. In the midst of suffering, it is strengthening to reclaim all that baptism promises, both in life and in death. So also at the time of death. Death fulfills our dying with Christ of which baptism is the sign. Forms of the reaffirmation of baptismal vows, such as the one on pages 117–120,[14] can be helpful in ministry with the sick and the dying in reclaiming the promises of baptism. If it seems more appropriate not to include the responses of the person who is ill, the significance of the vows may be included in the prayer of blessing.

## Ministry at the Time of Death

The pastoral care of the dying and of their families is a singularly important ministry of the church. When death comes, it comes as an enemy. Many have died repeating in their own fashion the words of Jesus on the cross: "My God, why have you forsaken me?" The illusion that the right medical technology will put things right is challenged by a dying patient's question: "Why is getting old and dying so painful?" Whenever the death occurs, the pastoral visitor will be careful to act in a manner appropriate to the occasion. In particular, the considerate visitor will respect the wishes of the dying person and the attending family members.

Nevertheless, for Christian faith, death is ultimately a defeated enemy. Christ has been raised from the dead, and it is not for this life only that we have hoped in Christ (1 Cor. 15:19). The pastoral care of the dying is the ministry of the risen Jesus Christ through his body, the church. In its ministry of pastoral care the church testifies to its baptismal faith, the faith that through Christ we have passed from death into life.

The commendation of the dying may be a simple blessing from scripture. Time and opportunity may also allow the reading of longer familiar passages and for prayers such as those provided on pages 123–128.[15]

The time immediately before dying can provide opportunity for transforming the emotional attachments of the present life. It can also allow for good conversation, farewells, forgiveness, expressions of affection, or a reassurance that affairs have been put in order.

Pastoral care is the ministry of Jesus Christ in and through his body, the church. As he answered John the Baptist's question with acts of healing, so the church today answers, by its ministry, the perennial question: "Is Jesus Christ the one who is to come, or shall we look for another?" In its ministry of pastoral care, the Christian church witnesses to its baptismal faith, that faith which can face all that life and death can present, for, "We have been buried with him by baptism into death, so that, just as Christ was raised from the dead . . . we too might walk in newness of life" (Rom. 6:4).

# MINISTRY WITH THE SICK

# SENTENCES OF SCRIPTURE

*The following sentences may be used as calls to worship or as introductions to prayer. An appropriate sentence may be selected and left with the person at the end of a visit.*

The eternal God is your dwelling place,
and underneath are the everlasting arms.                    *Deut. 33:27a*

Be strong and courageous;
do not be frightened or dismayed,
for the LORD your God is with you
wherever you go.                                            *Josh. 1:9b*

The LORD is my shepherd, I shall not want.
For you are with me;
your rod and your staff—they comfort me.                    *Ps. 23:1, 4b*

The LORD is my light and my salvation;
whom shall I fear?
The LORD is the stronghold of my life;
of whom shall I be afraid?                                  *Ps. 27:1*

For God will hide me in a shelter
in the day of trouble;
God will conceal me under the cover of a tent,
and will set me high on a rock.                             *Ps. 27:5*

God is our refuge and strength,
a very present help in trouble.                             *Ps. 46:1*

| Be still, and know that I am God! | *Ps. 46:10* |

Hear my prayer, O LORD;
let my cry come to you.
Do not hide your face from me
in the day of my distress.
Incline your ear to me;
answer me speedily in the day when I call.  *Ps. 102:1–2*

Our help is in the name of the LORD,
who made heaven and earth.  *Ps. 124:8*

Those of steadfast mind you keep in peace—
in peace because they trust in you.  *Isa. 26:3*

Those who wait for the LORD
shall renew their strength,
they shall mount up with wings like eagles,
they shall run and not be weary,
they shall walk and not faint.  *Isa. 40:31*

Do not fear, for I am with you,
do not be afraid, for I am your God;
I will strengthen you, I will help you,
I will uphold you with my victorious right hand.  *Isa. 41:10*

Come to me,
all you that are weary
and are carrying heavy burdens,
and I will give you rest.  *Matt. 11:28*

Let the children come to me,
do not stop them;
for it is to such as these that the kingdom
    of God belongs.  *Mark 10:14b*

I am the bread of life.
Whoever comes to me will never be hungry,
and whoever believes in me will never be thirsty.  *John 6:35*

I am the resurrection and the life.
Those who believe in me,
even though they die, will live,
and everyone who lives and believes in me
will never die.  *John 11:25–26*

Do not let your hearts be troubled.
Believe in God, believe also in me.                        *John 14:1*

Peace I leave with you;
my peace I give to you.
I do not give to you as the world gives.
Do not let your hearts be troubled,
and do not let them be afraid.                            *John 14:27*

I have said this to you,
so that in me you may have peace.
In the world you face persecution.
But take courage;
I have conquered the world!                              *John 16:33*

I consider that the sufferings of this present time
are not worth comparing
with the glory about to be revealed to us.               *Rom. 8:18*

God consoles us in all our affliction,
so that we may be able
to console those who are in any affliction.
For just as the sufferings of Christ are abundant
      for us,
so also our consolation is abundant through Christ.   *2 Cor. 1:4ab, 5*

My grace is sufficient for you,
for power is made perfect in weakness.                *2 Cor. 12:9a*

Give praise to God the Almighty,
by whose great mercy
we have been born anew to a living hope
through the resurrection of Jesus Christ from the dead.   *1 Peter 1:3*

Behold, I stand at the door and knock;
if you hear my voice and open the door,
I will come in to you and eat with you,
and you with me.                                        *Rev. 3:20*

# APPROPRIATE READINGS FROM SCRIPTURE

*The following readings are particularly appropriate for use in pastoral care. An asterisk (\*) indicates that the text of that particular reading is included in this resource (pp. 47–63).*

## Old Testament

| | |
|---|---|
| 1 Kings 19:4–8 | Elijah's despair in the wilderness |
| Job 5:7–11 | God sets on high those who are lowly |
| Job 7:11–21 | Job complains to God |
| Eccl. 3:1–15 | For everything there is a season |
| Isa. 26:1–4 | God will keep them in perfect peace |
| *Isa. 35 | The desert shall rejoice and blossom |
| Isa. 38 | Hezekiah's prayer in distress |
| Isa. 40:1–11 | Comfort my people |
| *Isa. 40:28–31 | Those who wait for the Lord shall renew their strength |
| Isa. 43:1–3a, 18–19, 25 | When you pass through the waters |
| Isa. 52:13—53:12 | Surely he has borne our grief |
| *Isa. 61:1–4 | The spirit of the Lord is upon me |

## Psalms

| | |
|---|---|
| *Ps. 6:2–4, 6–9 | Lord, heal me, my soul is struck with terror |
| *Ps. 22:1–2, 14–15, 19, 22–24 | My God, why have you forsaken me? |
| *Ps. 23 | The Lord is my shepherd |

| | |
|---|---|
| *Ps. 27:1, 4–9a, 13–14 | The Lord is my light and my salvation |
| Ps. 31:1–3, 5, 7, 16, 19, 24 | In this, O Lord, do I seek refuge |
| Ps. 34:1–10, 17–19, 22 | O magnify the Lord with me |
| Ps. 39:4–5, 12 | Lord, let me know my end |
| *Ps. 42:1–5 | As a deer longs for flowing streams |
| Ps. 46:1–5, 10–11 | A very present help in trouble |
| Ps. 51:1–12, 15–17 | Create in me a clean heart, O God |
| Ps. 63:1–8 | In the shadow of your wings, I sing for joy |
| *Ps. 69:1–3, 13–14a, 15–17, 29–30, 32–34 | Save me, for the waters come up to my neck |
| Ps. 71:1–3, 5–6, 8–9, 14–16 | Do not cast me off in the time of old age |
| Ps. 77 | I cry to God to hear me |
| *Ps. 86:1–7, 11–13, 15–16 | In the day of my trouble I call on you |
| Ps. 90:1–10, 12 | The eternity of God and human transitoriness |
| Ps. 91 | My refuge and my fortress, my God, in whom I trust |
| *Ps. 103:1–5 | Bless the Lord, O my soul |
| Ps. 116:1–9 | When I was brought low, the Lord saved me |
| *Ps. 121 | I lift up my eyes to the hills |
| *Ps. 130 | Out of the depths I cry to the Lord |
| Ps. 137:1–6 | By the rivers of Babylon |
| *Ps. 139:1–18, 23–24 | You have searched me and known me |
| Ps. 143:1–2, 5–6, 10 | Give ear to my supplications |

### New Testament

| | |
|---|---|
| *Matt. 5:1–12 | The Beatitudes |
| Matt. 8:14–17 | Jesus and Peter's mother-in-law |
| *Matt. 10:1, 5a, 7–8a; Mark 6:12–13 | Jesus calls disciples and sends them out |
| *Matt. 11:2–5 | Go and tell John what you hear and see |
| *Matt. 11:28–30 | All who labor and are heavy laden |
| Mark 6:53–56 | Healing in Gennesaret |
| *Mark 10:13–16 | Let the children come to me |
| Mark 15:24b–34 | My God, why have you forsaken me? |
| Luke 4:31–37 | The man with an unclean spirit |
| *Luke 4:40 | Jesus lays hands on the sick and heals them |

| | |
|---|---|
| *Luke 5:12–16 | A leper is cleansed |
| Luke 5:17–26 | Paralytic carried by four men |
| Luke 7:2–10 | The centurion's servant |
| Luke 8:26–35 | The demoniac(s) at Gadara |
| *Luke 8:43–48 | The woman with an issue of blood |
| Luke 9:37–43 | Epileptic boy |
| Luke 13:10–17 | Woman bent double for eighteen years |
| Luke 17:11–19 | The ten lepers |
| Luke 18:35–43 | Blind Bartimaeus |
| John 3:16–17 | God so loved the world |
| John 4:46–54 | The nobleman's son |
| John 5:2–18 | Sick man at pool of Bethesda |
| John 9:1–7 | Who sinned . . . that he was born blind? |
| John 10:11–18 | I am the good shepherd |
| *John 14:1–6, 25–27 | Let not your hearts be troubled |
| *Acts 3:1–10 | The lame man at the temple gate |
| Rom. 5:1–11 | Hope does not disappoint |
| *Rom. 8:14–23 | Present sufferings not wórth comparing with glory to be revealed |
| *Rom. 8:26–28 | The Spirit helps us in our weakness |
| *Rom. 8:31–39 | If God is for us, who is against us? |
| *Rom. 12:1, 2 | Present your bodies as a living sacrifice |
| 1 Cor. 12:24b–27 | The members may have the same care for one another |
| 2 Cor. 1:3–7 | Sharing in sufferings and in comfort |
| 2 Cor. 4:16–18 | Visible things are transitory, invisible things permanent |
| Phil. 2:25–30 | Epaphroditus' illness |
| *Phil. 4:4, 6–9 | Rejoice in the Lord always; have no anxiety |
| Heb. 2:14–18 | Christ was tempted in every way |
| *Heb. 4:14–16; 5:7–9 | Christ learned obedience through what he suffered |
| *James 5:13–16 | Is anyone among you suffering? |
| *1 Peter 1:3–9 | Born anew to a living hope |
| 1 John 3:1–3 | We are children of God |
| 1 John 4:16–19 | There is no fear in love |
| Rev. 21:1–7 | God will wipe away every tear |

# SELECTED SCRIPTURE READINGS

*All readings are from the New Revised Standard Version of the Bible.*

## Old Testament

*Isaiah 35*

The wilderness and the dry land shall be glad,
    the desert shall rejoice and blossom;
like the crocus it shall blossom abundantly,
    and rejoice with joy and singing.
The glory of Lebanon shall be given to it,
    the majesty of Carmel and Sharon.
They shall see the glory of the LORD,
    the majesty of our God.

Strengthen the weak hands,
    and make firm the feeble knees.
Say to those who are of a fearful heart,
    "Be strong, do not fear!
Here is your God.
    He will come with vengeance,
with terrible recompense.
    He will come and save you."

Then the eyes of the blind shall be opened,
　　and the ears of the deaf unstopped;
then the lame shall leap like a deer,
　　and the tongue of the speechless sing for joy.
For waters shall break forth in the wilderness,
　　and streams in the desert;
the burning sand shall become a pool,
　　and the thirsty ground springs of water;
the haunt of jackals shall become a swamp,
　　the grass shall become reeds and rushes.

A highway shall be there,
　　and it shall be called the Holy Way;
the unclean shall not travel on it,
　　　but it shall be for God's people;
　　no traveler, not even fools, shall go astray.
No lion shall be there,
　　nor shall any ravenous beast come up on it;
they shall not be found there,
　　but the redeemed shall walk there.
And the ransomed of the LORD shall return,
　　and come to Zion with singing;
everlasting joy shall be upon their heads;
　　they shall obtain joy and gladness,
　　and sorrow and sighing shall flee away.

*Isaiah 40:28–31*

Have you not known? Have you not heard?
The LORD is the everlasting God,
　　the Creator of the ends of the earth.
He does not faint or grow weary;
　　his understanding is unsearchable.
He gives power to the faint,
　　and strengthens the powerless.
Even youths will faint and be weary,
　　and the young will fall exhausted;
but those who wait for the LORD shall renew their strength,
　　they shall mount up with wings like eagles,
they shall run and not be weary,
　　they shall walk and not faint.

*Isaiah 61:1–4*

The spirit of the Lord GOD is upon me,
    because the LORD has anointed me;
he has sent me to bring good news to the oppressed,
    to bind up the brokenhearted,
to proclaim liberty to the captives,
    and release to the prisoners;
to proclaim the year of the LORD's favor,
    and the day of vengeance of our God;
    to comfort all who mourn;
to provide for those who mourn in Zion—
    to give them a garland instead of ashes,
the oil of gladness instead of mourning,
    the mantle of praise instead of a faint spirit.
They will be called oaks of righteousness,
    the planting of the LORD, to display his glory.
They shall build up the ancient ruins,
    they shall raise up the former devastations;
they shall repair the ruined cities,
    the devastations of many generations.

## Psalms

*Psalm 6:2–4, 6–9*

Be gracious to me, O LORD, for I am languishing;
    O LORD, heal me, for my bones are shaking with terror.
My soul also is struck with terror,
    while you, O LORD—how long?

Turn, O LORD, save my life;
    deliver me for the sake of your steadfast love.

I am weary with my moaning;
    every night I flood my bed with tears;
    I drench my couch with my weeping.
My eyes waste away because of grief;
    they grow weak because of all my foes.

Depart from me, all you workers of evil,
  for the LORD has heard the sound of my weeping.
The LORD has heard my supplication;
  the LORD accepts my prayer.

*Psalm 22:1–2, 14–15, 19, 22–24*

My God, my God, why have you forsaken me?
  Why are you so far from helping me, from the words of my
    groaning?
O my God, I cry by day, but you do not answer;
  and by night, but find no rest.

I am poured out like water,
  and all my bones are out of joint;
my heart is like wax;
  it is melted within my breast;
my mouth is dried up like a potsherd,
  and my tongue sticks to my jaws;
  you lay me in the dust of death.

But you, O LORD, do not be far away!
  O my help, come quickly to my aid!

I will tell of your name to my brothers and sisters;
  in the midst of the congregation I will praise you:
You who fear the LORD, praise him!
  All you offspring of Jacob, glorify him;
  stand in awe of him, all you offspring of Israel!
For he did not despise or abhor
  the affliction of the afflicted;
he did not hide his face from me,
  but heard when I cried to him.

*Psalm 23*

The LORD is my shepherd, I shall not want.
  He makes me lie down in green pastures;
he leads me beside still waters;
  he restores my soul.
He leads me in right paths
  for his name's sake.

Even though I walk through the darkest valley,
   I fear no evil;
for you are with me;
   your rod and your staff—
   they comfort me.

You prepare a table before me
   in the presence of my enemies;
you anoint my head with oil;
   my cup overflows.
Surely goodness and mercy shall follow me
   all the days of my life,
and I shall dwell in the house of the LORD
   my whole life long.


   *Psalm 27:1, 4–9a, 13–14*

The LORD is my light and my salvation;
   whom shall I fear?
The LORD is the stronghold of my life;
   of whom shall I be afraid?

One thing I asked of the LORD,
   that I will seek after:
to live in the house of the LORD
   all the days of my life,
to behold the beauty of the LORD,
   and to inquire in his temple.

For he will hide me in his shelter
   in the day of trouble;
he will conceal me under the cover of his tent;
   he will set me high on a rock.

Now my head is lifted up
   above my enemies all around me,
and I will offer in his tent
   sacrifices with shouts of joy;
I will sing and make melody to the LORD.

Hear, O LORD, when I cry aloud,
   be gracious to me and answer me!
"Come," my heart says, "seek his face!"
   Your face, LORD, do I seek.
   Do not hide your face from me.

I believe that I shall see the goodness of the LORD
   in the land of the living.
Wait for the LORD;
   be strong, and let your heart take courage;
   wait for the LORD!

   *Psalm 42:1–5*

As a deer longs for flowing streams,
   so my soul longs for you, O God.
My soul thirsts for God,
   for the living God.
When shall I come and behold
   the face of God?
My tears have been my food
   day and night,
while people say to me continually,
   "Where is your God?"

These things I remember,
   as I pour out my soul:
how I went with the throng,
   and led them in procession to the house of God,
with glad shouts and songs of thanksgiving,
   a multitude keeping festival.
Why are you cast down, O my soul,
   and why are you disquieted within me?
Hope in God; for I shall again praise him,
   my help and my God.

*Psalm 69:1–3, 13–14a, 15–17, 29–30, 32–34*

Save me, O God,
    for the waters have come up to my neck.
I sink in deep mire,
    where there is no foothold;
I have come into deep waters,
    and the flood sweeps over me.
I am weary with my crying;
    my throat is parched.
My eyes grow dim
    with waiting for my God.

But as for me, my prayer is to you, O LORD.
    At an acceptable time, O God,
    in the abundance of your steadfast love, answer me.
With your faithful help rescue me
    from sinking in the mire.

Do not let the flood sweep over me,
    or the deep swallow me up,
    or the Pit close its mouth over me.

Answer me, O LORD, for your steadfast love is good;
    according to your abundant mercy, turn to me.
Do not hide your face from your servant,
    for I am in distress—make haste to answer me.

But I am lowly and in pain;
    let your salvation, O God, protect me.

I will praise the name of God with a song;
    I will magnify him with thanksgiving.

Let the oppressed see it and be glad;
    you who seek God, let your hearts revive.
For the LORD hears the needy,
    and does not despise his own that are in bonds.

Let heaven and earth praise him,
    the seas and everything that moves in them.

*Psalm 86:1–7, 11–13, 15–16*

Incline your ear, O LORD, and answer me,
    for I am poor and needy.
Preserve my life, for I am devoted to you;
    save your servant who trusts in you.
You are my God; be gracious to me, O Lord,
    for to you do I cry all day long.
Gladden the soul of your servant,
    for to you, O Lord, I lift up my soul.
For you, O Lord, are good and forgiving,
    abounding in steadfast love to all who call on you.
Give ear, O LORD, to my prayer;
    listen to my cry of supplication.
In the day of my trouble I call on you,
    for you will answer me.

Teach me your way, O LORD,
    that I may walk in your truth;
    give me an undivided heart to revere your name.
I give thanks to you, O Lord my God, with my whole heart,
    and I will glorify your name forever.
For great is your steadfast love toward me;
    you have delivered my soul from the depths of Sheol.

But you, O Lord, are a God merciful and gracious,
    slow to anger and abounding in steadfast love and faithfulness.
Turn to me and be gracious to me;
    give your strength to your servant;
    save the child of your serving girl.

*Psalm 103:1–5*

Bless the LORD, O my soul,
    and all that is within me,
    bless his holy name.
Bless the LORD, O my soul,
    and do not forget all his benefits—
who forgives all your iniquity,
    who heals all your diseases,
who redeems your life from the Pit,
    who crowns you with steadfast love and mercy,
who satisfies you with good as long as you live
    so that your youth is renewed like the eagle's.

*Psalm 121*

I lift up my eyes to the hills—
    from where will my help come?
My help comes from the LORD,
    who made heaven and earth.

He will not let your foot be moved;
    he who keeps you will not slumber.
He who keeps Israel
    will neither slumber nor sleep.

The LORD is your keeper;
    the LORD is your shade at your right hand.
The sun shall not strike you by day,
    nor the moon by night.

The LORD will keep you from all evil;
    he will keep your life.
The LORD will keep
    your going out and your coming in
    from this time on and forevermore.

*Psalm 130*

Out of the depths I cry to you, O LORD.
    Lord, hear my voice!
Let your ears be attentive
    to the voice of my supplications!

If you, O LORD, should mark iniquities,
    Lord, who could stand?
But there is forgiveness with you,
    so that you may be revered.

I wait for the LORD, my soul waits,
    and in his word I hope;
my soul waits for the LORD
    more than those who watch for the morning,
    more than those who watch for the morning.

O Israel, hope in the LORD!
　　For with the LORD there is steadfast love,
　　and with him is great power to redeem.
It is he who will redeem Israel
　　from all its iniquities.

*Psalm 139:1–18, 23–24*

O LORD, you have searched me and known me.
You know when I sit down and when I rise up;
　　you discern my thoughts from far away.
You search out my path and my lying down,
　　and are acquainted with all my ways.
Even before a word is on my tongue,
　　O LORD, you know it completely.
You hem me in, behind and before,
　　and lay your hand upon me.
Such knowledge is too wonderful for me;
　　it is so high that I cannot attain it.

Where can I go from your spirit?
　　Or where can I flee from your presence?
If I ascend to heaven, you are there;
　　if I make my bed in Sheol, you are there.
If I take the wings of the morning
　　and settle at the farthest limits of the sea,
even there your hand shall lead me,
　　and your right hand shall hold me fast.
If I say, "Surely the darkness shall cover me,
　　and the light around me become night,"
even the darkness is not dark to you;
　　the night is as bright as the day,
　　for darkness is as light to you.

For it was you who formed my inward parts;
　　you knit me together in my mother's womb.
I praise you, for I am fearfully and wonderfully made.
　　Wonderful are your works;
that I know very well.
　　My frame was not hidden from you,
when I was being made in secret,
　　intricately woven in the depths of the earth.

Your eyes beheld my unformed substance.
In your book were written
  all the days that were formed for me,
  when none of them as yet existed.
How weighty to me are your thoughts, O God!
  How vast is the sum of them!
I try to count them—they are more than the sand;
  I come to the end—I am still with you.

Search me, O God, and know my heart;
  test me and know my thoughts.
See if there is any wicked way in me,
  and lead me in the way everlasting.

## New Testament

*Matthew 5:1–12*

When Jesus saw the crowds, he went up the mountain; and after he sat down, his disciples came to him. Then he began to speak, and taught them, saying:
  "Blessed are the poor in spirit, for theirs is the kingdom of heaven.
  "Blessed are those who mourn, for they will be comforted.
  "Blessed are the meek, for they will inherit the earth.
  "Blessed are those who hunger and thirst for righteousness, for they will be filled.
  "Blessed are the merciful, for they will receive mercy.
  "Blessed are the pure in heart, for they will see God.
  "Blessed are the peacemakers, for they will be called children of God.
  "Blessed are those who are persecuted for righteousness' sake, for theirs is the kingdom of heaven.
  "Blessed are you when people revile you and persecute you and utter all kinds of evil against you falsely on my account. Rejoice and be glad, for your reward is great in heaven, for in the same way they persecuted the prophets who were before you."

*Matthew 10:1, 5a, 7–8a; Mark 6:12–13*

Jesus summoned his twelve disciples and gave them authority over unclean spirits, to cast them out, and to cure every disease and every sickness. These twelve Jesus sent out with the following instructions: "As you go, proclaim the good news, 'The kingdom of heaven has come near.' Cure the sick." So they went out and proclaimed that all should repent. They cast out many demons, and anointed with oil many who were sick and cured them.

*Matthew 11:2–5*

When John heard in prison what the Messiah was doing, he sent word by his disciples and said to him, "Are you the one who is to come, or are we to wait for another?" Jesus answered them, "Go and tell John what you hear and see: the blind receive their sight, the lame walk, the lepers are cleansed, the deaf hear, the dead are raised, and the poor have good news brought to them."

*Matthew 11:28–30*

Come to me, all you that are weary and are carrying heavy burdens, and I will give you rest. Take my yoke upon you, and learn from me; for I am gentle and humble in heart, and you will find rest for your souls. For my yoke is easy, and my burden is light.

*Mark 10:13–16*

People were bringing little children to [Jesus] in order that he might touch them; and the disciples spoke sternly to them. But when Jesus saw this, he was indignant and said to them, "Let the little children come to me; do not stop them; for it is to such as these that the kingdom of God belongs. Truly I tell you, whoever does not receive the kingdom of God as a little child will never enter it." And he took them up in his arms, laid his hands on them, and blessed them.

*Luke 4:40*

As the sun was setting, all those who had any who were sick with various kinds of diseases brought them to [Jesus]; and he laid his hands on each of them and cured them.

*Luke 5:12–16*

Once, when [Jesus] was in one of the cities, there was a man covered with leprosy. When he saw Jesus, he bowed with his face to the ground and begged him, "Lord, if you choose, you can make me clean." Then Jesus stretched out his hand, touched him, and said, "I do choose. Be made clean." Immediately the leprosy left him. And he ordered him to tell no one. "Go," he said, "and show yourself to the priest, and, as Moses commanded, make an offering for your cleansing, for a testimony to them." But now more than ever the word about Jesus spread abroad; many crowds would gather to hear him and to be cured of their diseases. But he would withdraw to deserted places and pray.

*Luke 8:43–48*

Now there was a woman who had been suffering from hemorrhages for twelve years; and though she had spent all she had on physicians, no one could cure her. She came up behind [Jesus] and touched the fringe of his clothes, and immediately her hemorrhage stopped. Then Jesus asked, "Who touched me?" When all denied it, Peter said, "Master, the crowds surround you and press in on you." But Jesus said, "Someone touched me; for I noticed that power had gone out from me." When the woman saw that she could not remain hidden, she came trembling; and falling down before him, she declared in the presence of all the people why she had touched him, and how she had been immediately healed. He said to her, "Daughter, your faith has made you well; go in peace."

*John 14:1–6, 25–27*

"Do not let your hearts be troubled. Believe in God, believe also in me. In my Father's house there are many dwelling places. If it were not so, would I have told you that I go to prepare a place for you? And if I go and prepare a place for you, I will come again and will take you to myself, so that where I am, there you may be also. And you know the way to the place where I am going." Thomas said to him, "Lord, we do not know where you are going. How can we know the way?" Jesus said to him, "I am the way, and the truth, and the life. No one comes to the Father, except through me.

"I have said these things to you while I am still with you. But the Advocate, the Holy Spirit, whom the Father will send in my name, will teach you everything, and remind you of all that I have said to you. Peace I leave with you; my peace I give to you. I do not give to you as the world gives. Do not let your hearts be troubled, and do not let them be afraid."

*Acts 3:1–10*

One day Peter and John were going up to the temple at the hour of prayer, at three o'clock in the afternoon. And a man lame from birth was being carried in. People would lay him daily at the gate of the temple called the Beautiful Gate so that he could ask for alms from those entering the temple. When he saw Peter and John about to go into the temple, he asked them for alms. Peter looked intently at him, as John did, and said, "Look at us." And he fixed his attention on them, expecting to receive something from them. But Peter said, "I have no silver or gold, but what I have I give you; in the name of Jesus Christ of Nazareth, stand up and walk." And he took him by the right hand and raised him up; and immediately his feet and ankles were made strong. Jumping up, he stood and began to walk, and he entered the temple with them, walking and leaping and praising God. All the people saw him walking and praising God, and they recognized him as the one who used to sit and ask for alms at the Beautiful Gate of the temple; and they were filled with wonder and amazement at what had happened to him.

*Romans 8:14–23*

For all who are led by the Spirit of God are children of God. For you did not receive a spirit of slavery to fall back into fear, but you have received a spirit of adoption. When we cry, "Abba! Father!" it is that very Spirit bearing witness with our spirit that we are children of God, and if children, then heirs, heirs of God and joint heirs with Christ—if, in fact, we suffer with him so that we may also be glorified with him.

I consider that the sufferings of this present time are not worth comparing with the glory about to be revealed to us. For the creation waits with eager longing for the revealing of the children of God; for the creation was subjected to futility, not of its own will but by the will of the one who subjected it, in hope that the creation itself will be set free from its bondage to decay and will obtain the freedom of the glory of the children of God. We know that the whole creation has been groaning in labor pains until now; and not only the creation, but we ourselves, who have the first fruits of the Spirit, groan inwardly while we wait for adoption, the redemption of our bodies.

*Romans 8:26–28*

Likewise the Spirit helps us in our weakness; for we do not know how to pray as we ought, but that very Spirit intercedes with sighs too deep for words. And God, who searches the heart, knows what is the mind of the Spirit, because the Spirit intercedes for the saints according to the will of God. We know that all things work together for good for those who love God, who are called according to his purpose.

*Romans 8:31–39*

What then are we to say about these things? If God is for us, who is against us? He who did not withhold his own Son, but gave him up for all of us, will he not with him also give us everything else? Who will bring any charge against God's elect? It is God who justifies. Who is to condemn? It is Christ Jesus, who died, yes, who was raised, who is at the right hand of God, who indeed intercedes for us. Who will separate us from the love of Christ? Will hardship, or distress, or persecution, or famine, or nakedness, or peril, or sword? As it is written,

> "For your sake we are being killed all day long;
> we are counted as sheep to be slaughtered."

No, in all these things we are more than conquerors through him who loved us. For I am convinced that neither death, nor life, nor angels, nor rulers, nor things present, nor things to come, nor powers, nor height, nor depth, nor anything else in all creation, will be able to separate us from the love of God in Christ Jesus our Lord.

*Romans 12:1, 2*

I appeal to you therefore, brothers and sisters, by the mercies of God, to present your bodies as a living sacrifice, holy and acceptable to God, which is your spiritual worship. Do not be conformed to this world, but be transformed by the renewing of your minds, so that you may discern what is the will of God—what is good and acceptable and perfect.

*Philippians 4:4, 6–9*

Rejoice in the Lord always; again I will say, Rejoice. Do not worry about anything, but in everything by prayer and supplication with thanksgiving let your requests be made known to God. And the peace of God, which surpasses all understanding, will guard your hearts and your minds in Christ Jesus.

Finally, beloved, whatever is true, whatever is honorable, whatever is just, whatever is pure, whatever is pleasing, whatever is commendable, if there is any excellence, and if there is anything worthy of praise, think about these things. Keep on doing the things that you have learned and received and heard and seen in me, and the God of peace will be with you.

*Hebrews 4:14–16; 5:7–9*

Since, then, we have a great high priest who has passed through the heavens, Jesus, the Son of God, let us hold fast to our confession. For we do not have a high priest who is unable to sympathize with our weaknesses, but we have one who in every respect has been tested as we are, yet without sin. Let us therefore approach the throne of grace with boldness, so that we may receive mercy and find grace to help in time of need.

In the days of his flesh, Jesus offered up prayers and supplications, with loud cries and tears, to the one who was able to save him from death, and he was heard because of his reverent submission. Although he was a Son, he learned obedience through what he suffered; and having been made perfect, he became the source of eternal salvation for all who obey him.

*James 5:13–16*

Are any among you suffering? They should pray. Are any cheerful? They should sing songs of praise. Are any among you sick? They should call for the elders of the church and have them pray over them, anointing them with oil in the name of the Lord. The prayer of faith will save the sick, and the Lord will raise them up; and anyone who has committed sins will be forgiven. Therefore confess your sins to one another, and pray for one another, so that you may be healed. The prayer of the righteous is powerful and effective.

*1 Peter 1:3–9*

Blessed be the God and Father of our Lord Jesus Christ! By his great mercy he has given us a new birth into a living hope through the resurrection of Jesus Christ from the dead, and into an inheritance that is imperishable, undefiled, and unfading, kept in heaven for you, who are being protected by the power of God through faith for a salvation ready to be revealed in the last time. In this you rejoice, even if now for a little while you have had to suffer various trials, so that the genuineness of your faith—being more precious than gold that, though perishable, is tested by fire—may be found to result in praise and glory and honor when Jesus Christ is revealed. Although you have not seen him, you love him; and even though you do not see him now, you believe in him and rejoice with an indescribable and glorious joy, for you are receiving the outcome of your faith, the salvation of your souls.

# PRAYERS

*These prayers may be used in visitations with the sick and in the services that follow in this book. They may also suggest language or theme for extemporary prayer when that form of prayer is more suitable.*

**1**

*For the sick*

Lord of all health,
you are the source of our life
and our fulfillment in death.
Be for _____ now
comfort in the midst of pain,
strength to transform weakness,
and light to brighten darkness,
through Christ our Lord.

**Amen.**

**2**

*For healing*

By your power, great God,
our Lord Jesus healed the sick
and gave new hope to the hopeless.
Though we cannot command or possess your power,
we pray for those who want to be healed
(especially for _____).

Mend their wounds, soothe fevered brows,
and make broken people whole again.
Help us to welcome every healing as a sign that,
though death is against us,
you are for us,
and have promised renewed and risen life
in Jesus Christ the Lord.

**Amen.**

3

*For parents of a sick child*

Merciful God,
enfold _____ [name of child] in the arms of your love.
Comfort _____ [parents] in their anxiety.
Deliver them from despair,
give them patience to endure,
and guide them to choose wisely for _____ [name of child],
in the name of him who welcomed little children,
even Jesus Christ our Lord.

**Amen.**

4

*For those experiencing tragedy*

Out of the darkness we cry to you, O God.
Enable us to find in Christ
the faith to trust your care
even in the midst of pain,
so that we may not walk alone
through the valley of the shadow of death;
through Christ our Lord.

**Amen.**

5

*For a sick child*

Jesus, friend of little children,
bless _____ with your healing love
and make *him/her* well.

**Amen.**

**6**

*For the sick and those giving care*

Faithful Healer of the sick,
in your loving mercy,
embrace _____ in *her/his* time of need.
Guide the nurses, doctors,
and others who attend *her/him*.
Use their skills
to restore _____ to health and joy
for the service of Christ our Savior.

**Amen.**

**7**

*For those who work for healing*

God of compassion,
who in Jesus Christ healed the sick,
bless all who continue your work of healing.
Enhance their skills, and deepen their understanding,
that through their ministry
those who suffer may be restored to fullness of health,
for the sake of Christ our Lord.

**Amen.**

**8**

*For those in medical services*

Merciful God,
your healing power is everywhere about us.
Strengthen those who work among the sick;
give them courage and confidence in everything they do.
Encourage them when their efforts seem futile
or when death prevails.
Increase their trust in your power
even to overcome death and pain and crying.
May they be thankful for every sign of health you give,
and humble before the mystery of your healing grace;
through Jesus Christ our Lord.

**Amen.**

**9**

*For one in emotional distress*

Merciful God,
you give us the grace that helps in time of need.
Surround _____ with your steadfast love
and lighten *his/her* burden.
By the power of your Spirit,
free *him/her* from distress
and give *him/her* a new mind and heart made whole
in the name of the risen Christ.

**Amen.**

**10**

*For one in emotional distress*

God of life,
deliver your servant _____
from distress and loneliness.
Give *her/him* your peace
and fill *her/him* with your Holy Spirit.
Lift *her/him* from despair
to claim the life you offer in Jesus Christ,
in whose name we pray.

**Amen.**

**11**

*For those in mental distress*

Mighty God,
in Jesus Christ you deal with spirits that darken our minds
and set us against ourselves.
Give peace to those who are torn by conflict,
cast down, or lost in worlds of illusion.
By your power,
drive from our minds demons that shake confidence
and wreck love.
Tame unruly forces within us
and bring us to your truth,

so that we may accept ourselves
as your beloved children in Jesus Christ.

**Amen.**

12

*For one who has attempted suicide*

Gracious God,
your Son came among us not to condemn but to save.
He taught us that nothing can separate us from your love.
Release us from the fear that we are worthless
and stay our hands from self-destruction.
Uphold _____ with your love.
Fill *him/her* with hope
and with trust in your guidance,
that your power may make *him/her* new
through the grace of our Lord Jesus Christ.

**Amen.**

13

*For one who is anxious*

Merciful God,
in Jesus Christ we have your promise of peace.
Receive _____, who seeks your help.
Assure *her/him* that you are near.
Fill *her/him* with your Spirit,
cast out *her/his* anxiety and fear,
and help *her/him* to rely on the strength you provide;
through Jesus Christ our Lord.

**Amen.**

14

*For someone who is old*

God of grace and hope,
we thank you for life, love, and good memories,
for the gift of age,
and for the wisdom that comes from experience.
We bless you for your constant presence,
for with you there is fullness of joy.

Give us the courage and faith
to accept life as it comes,
confident that the future is yours
and that we belong to you forever;
through Jesus Christ our Lord.

**Amen.**

### 15
*For those in coma or unable to communicate*

Eternal God,
you have known us before we were here
and will continue to know us after we are gone.
Touch _____ with your grace and presence.
As you give your abiding care,
assure *him/her* of our love and presence.
Though we are unable to respond to each other,
assure *him/her* that our communion together remains secure
and your love for *him/her* is unfailing.
In Christ, who came through to us, we pray.

**Amen.**

### 16
*For a patient with Alzheimer's disease*

God of compassion,
you have borne our griefs
and carried our sorrows.
Preserve your covenant of peace
with your servant, _____, in *her/his* distress.
Although the pain of *her/his* forgetfulness is great,
we rejoice that you remember *her/him* always in your grace.
Supply *her/his* every need
according to the riches of your glory in Christ Jesus.

**Amen.**

### 17
*For those giving care to a patient with Alzheimer's disease*

God, our refuge and strength,
our present help in time of trouble,
care for those who tend the needs of _____.

Strengthen them in body and spirit.
Refresh them when weary;
console them when anxious;
comfort them in grief;
and hearten them in discouragement.
Lord of peace,
be with us all
and give us peace at all times
and in every way.

**Amen.**

18

*For use when a life-support system is withdrawn*

God of compassion and love,
you have breathed into us the breath of life
and have given us the exercise of our minds and wills.
In our frailty we surrender all life to you from whom it came,
trusting in your gracious promises;
through Jesus Christ our Lord.

**Amen.**

19

*For parents after the birth of a stillborn child or the death of a newly born child*

Merciful God,
you strengthen us by your power and wisdom.
Be gracious to _____ and _____ in their grief,
and surround them with your unfailing love;
that they may not be overwhelmed by their loss,
but have confidence in your goodness,
and courage to meet the days to come;
through Jesus Christ our Lord.

**Amen.**

# HOLY COMMUNION
# WITH THOSE UNABLE
# TO ATTEND PUBLIC WORSHIP

# OUTLINE OF HOLY COMMUNION WITH THOSE UNABLE TO ATTEND PUBLIC WORSHIP

Call to Worship
[Psalm, Hymn, or Spiritual Song]
[Confession of Sin]
[Declaration of Pardon]
Scripture Reading and Brief Sermon
Invitation to the Lord's Supper
Great Prayer of Thanksgiving
    concluding with the Lord's Prayer
Breaking of the Bread
    with Words of Institution
Communion
Prayer After Communion
Blessing

## WITH OPTION OF LAYING ON OF HANDS [AND ANOINTING]

Call to Worship
[Doxology, Psalm, Hymn, or Spiritual Song]
[Confession of Sin]
[Declaration of Pardon]
Scripture Reading and Brief Sermon
[Laying On of Hands]
[Anointing]
[Psalm, Hymn, or Spiritual Song]
Invitation to the Lord's Supper
Great Prayer of Thanksgiving
    concluding with the Lord's Prayer
Breaking of the Bread
    with Words of Institution
Communion
Prayer After Communion
Blessing

# HOLY COMMUNION
# WITH THOSE UNABLE
# TO ATTEND PUBLIC WORSHIP

*The minister shall be accompanied by one or more members of the congregation authorized by the session to represent the church.*

## CALL TO WORSHIP

*The minister says:*

The peace of the Lord be always with you.

**And also with you.**

*And*

Jesus says:
Come to me,
all you that are weary and are carrying heavy burdens,
and I will give you rest.
Take my yoke upon you, and learn from me;
for I am gentle and humble in heart,
and you will find rest for your souls.                    *Matt. 11:28–29*

*Or*

I am the bread of life.
Whoever comes to me will never be hungry,
and whoever believes in me will never be thirsty.
Everything that the Father gives me will come to me,
and anyone who comes to me I will never drive away. *John 6:35, 37*

*Or*

For where two or three are gathered in my name,
I am there among them.                                   *Matt. 18:20*

*Or*

Blessed are those who hunger and thirst for righteousness,
for they will be filled.                                 *Matt. 5:6*

*Or*

Behold, I stand at the door and knock;
if you hear my voice and open the door,
I will come in to you and eat with you,
and you with me.                                                                                                    *Rev. 3:20*

*A doxology, a psalm, a hymn, or a spiritual song may be sung or said.*

## Confession of Sin

*The minister says:*

In the Lord's Supper,
Christ is present by the power of the Holy Spirit
and offers us his body, broken for our sake,
and his blood, shed for the forgiveness of our sins.

As we prepare to receive this great gift,
let us confess our sin
and hear the promise of forgiveness.

**Merciful God,
we confess that we have sinned against you
in thought, word, and deed,
by what we have done,
and by what we have left undone.
We have not loved you
with our whole heart and mind and strength;
we have not loved our neighbors as ourselves.
In your mercy forgive what we have been,
help us amend what we are,
and direct what we shall be,
so that we may delight in your will
and walk in your ways,
to the glory of your holy name. Amen.**

*The people may pray silently.*

## DECLARATION OF PARDON

*Then the minister says:*

The mercy of the Lord
is from everlasting to everlasting.
I declare to you, in the name of Jesus Christ,
you (we) are forgiven.

May the God of mercy,
who forgives you (us) all your (our) sins,
strengthen you (us) in all goodness
and by the power of the Holy Spirit
keep you (us) in eternal life.

**Amen.**

## SCRIPTURE READING AND BRIEF SERMON

*A scripture lesson shall be read and briefly interpreted.*

*Laying on of hands and anointing with oil may follow according to the service for wholeness (pp. 92–96).*

*A psalm, a hymn, or a spiritual song may be sung.*

## INVITATION TO THE LORD'S SUPPER

*The minister says:*

According to Luke,
when our risen Lord was at table with his disciples,
he took the bread, and blessed and broke it,
and gave it to them.
Then their eyes were opened
and they recognized him.                          *Luke 24:30–31*

## GREAT PRAYER OF THANKSGIVING

*The following may be said:*

The Lord be with you.

**And also with you.**

Lift up your hearts.

**We lift them to the Lord.**

Let us give thanks to the Lord our God.

**It is right to give our thanks and praise.**

*Then the minister says:*

Holy God, we praise you.
Let the heavens be joyful
and the earth be glad.

We bless you for creating the whole world,
for your promises to your people Israel,
and for the life we have from Jesus Christ,
in whom your fullness dwells.

Born of Mary, he shares our life.
Eating with sinners, he welcomes us.
Leading your followers, he guides us.
Visiting the sick, he heals us.
Dying on the cross, he saves us.
Risen from the dead, he gives new life.
Living with you, he prays for us.

[Therefore we praise you,
joining our voice with choirs of angels,
and with all the faithful of every time and place,
who forever sing to the glory of your name:

**Holy, holy, holy Lord, God of power and might,
heaven and earth are full of your glory.**
  **Hosanna in the highest.**

**Blessed is he who comes in the name of the Lord.**
  **Hosanna in the highest.]**

With thanksgiving we take this bread and this cup
and proclaim the death and resurrection of our Lord.
Receive our sacrifice of praise.
Send to us your Holy Spirit,
that this meal may be holy
and your people may become one.
Unite us in faith,
inspire us to love,
encourage us with hope,
that we may receive Christ,
who comes to us in this holy banquet.

We praise you, eternal God,
through Christ your Word made flesh,
in the holy and life-giving Spirit.

**Amen.**

## THE LORD'S PRAYER

*The Lord's Prayer may be said.*

As our Savior Christ has taught us,
we now pray:

*Or*

| | |
|---|---|
| **Our Father in heaven,** | **Our Father, who art in heaven,** |
| **hallowed be your name,** | **hallowed be thy name,** |
| **your kingdom come,** | **thy kingdom come,** |
| **your will be done,** | **thy will be done,** |
| **on earth as in heaven.** | **on earth as it is in heaven.** |
| **Give us today our daily bread.** | **Give us this day our daily bread;** |
| **Forgive us our sins** | **and forgive us our debts,** |
| **as we forgive those who sin** | **as we forgive our debtors;** |
| **against us.** | **and lead us not into temptation,** |
| **Save us from the time of trial** | **but deliver us from evil.** |
| **and deliver us from evil.** | **For thine is the kingdom,** |
| **For the kingdom, the power,** | **and the power, and the glory,** |
| **and the glory are yours** | **forever.** |
| **now and for ever. Amen.** | **Amen.** |

## BREAKING OF THE BREAD

*The minister breaks the bread, saying:*

The Lord Jesus,
on the night of his arrest,
took bread,
and after giving thanks to God,
he broke it and said,
"This is my body, given for you.
Do this in remembrance of me."

*The minister lifts the cup, saying:*

In the same way,
he took the cup after supper, saying,
"This cup is the new covenant sealed in my blood.
Whenever you drink it,
do it in remembrance of me."

Every time you eat this bread and drink this cup,
you proclaim the death of the Lord, until he comes.     *1 Cor. 11:23–26*

## COMMUNION

*As the bread is given, the following may be said:*

_____ , the body of Christ, the bread of heaven.

**Amen.**

*Or*

_____ , the body of Christ given for you.

**Amen.**

*As the cup is given, the following may be said:*

_____ , the blood of Christ, the cup of salvation.

**Amen.**

_____, the blood of Christ shed for you.

**Amen.**

### PRAYER AFTER COMMUNION

*After all are served, the minister says:*

Let us pray.

We thank you, O God,
that through word and sacrament
you have given us your Son
who is the true bread of heaven
and food of eternal life.
So strengthen us in your service
that our daily living may show our thanks,
through Jesus Christ our Lord.

**Amen.**

### BLESSING

The Lord bless you and keep you.
The Lord be kind and gracious to you.
The Lord look upon you with favor
and give you peace.                                    *Num. 6:24–26*

**Amen.**

*Or*

The grace of our Lord Jesus Christ be with you.        *2 Thess. 3:18*

**Amen.**

# SERVICE FOR WHOLENESS

# OUTLINE OF A SERVICE FOR WHOLENESS FOR USE WITH A CONGREGATION

Opening Sentences
Psalm, Hymn, or Spiritual Song
Confession of Sin
Declaration of Pardon
Response (Psalm, Hymn, or Spiritual Song)
Prayer for Illumination
Scripture Readings
Sermon
[Psalm, Hymn, or Spiritual Song]
Offering of Our Lives to God
Intercession for Healing
Laying On of Hands and Anointing with Oil
   Thanksgiving and Invocation
   Lord's Prayer
   Laying On of Hands
   [Anointing with Oil]
   Prayer
   Dismissal
[Hymn]
Blessing

# OUTLINE OF A SERVICE FOR WHOLENESS
# WITH THE LORD'S SUPPER
# FOR USE WITH A CONGREGATION

*Celebration of the Lord's Supper may be included in the Service of Wholeness, following the thanksgiving and the dismissal of those who have received the laying on of hands (and anointing). The Lord's Prayer and the blessing are then omitted from the Service of Wholeness.*

Opening Sentences
Psalm, Hymn, or Spiritual Song
Confession of Sin
Declaration of Pardon
Response (Psalm, Hymn, or Spiritual Song)
Prayer for Illumination
Scripture Readings
Sermon
[Psalm, Hymn, or Spiritual Song]
Offering of Our Lives to God
Intercession for Healing
Laying On of Hands and Anointing with Oil
   Thanksgiving and Invocation
   Lord's Prayer
   Laying On of Hands
   [Anointing with Oil]
   Prayer
   Dismissal
[Hymn]
Invitation to the Lord's Supper
Great Prayer of Thanksgiving
   concluding with the Lord's Prayer
Breaking of Bread
   with Words of Institution
Communion
Prayer After Communion
Blessing

# OUTLINE OF A SERVICE FOR WHOLENESS FOLLOWING THE SERVICE FOR THE LORD'S DAY FOR USE WITH A CONGREGATION

*When the Service for Wholeness follows a service that included confession of sin, the reading of scripture, and a sermon, this service may omit those elements as follows.*

Opening Sentences
[Psalm, Hymn, or Spiritual Song]
Offering of Our Lives to God
Intercession for Healing
Laying On of Hands and Anointing with Oil
   Thanksgiving and Invocation
   Lord's Prayer
   Laying On of Hands
   [Anointing with Oil]
   Prayer
   Dismissal
[Hymn]
Blessing

# SERVICE FOR WHOLENESS
# FOR USE WITH A CONGREGATION

*The people are called to worship in these or similar words from scripture:*

Our help is in the name of the LORD,

**who made heaven and earth.** *Ps. 124:8*

*And one of the following:*

Those who wait for the LORD
shall renew their strength,
they shall mount up with wings like eagles,
they shall run and not be weary,
they shall walk and not faint. *Isa. 40:31*

Or

Give praise to God the Almighty,
by whose great mercy
we have been born anew to a living hope
through the resurrection of Jesus Christ from the dead. *1 Peter 1:3*

Or

God consoles us in all our affliction,
so that we may be able
to console those who are in any affliction.
For just as the sufferings of Christ are abundant for us,
so also our consolation is abundant through Christ. *2 Cor. 1:4ab, 5*

*A psalm, a hymn, or a spiritual song is sung.*

*When this service follows one that included confession of sin, the reading of scripture, and a sermon, continue on page 90.*

## CONFESSION OF SIN

*The people are called to confession with these or other sentences of scripture that promise God's forgiveness.*

Jesus said:
Ask, and it will be given you;
search, and you will find;
knock, and the door will be opened for you.

**For everyone who asks receives,**
**and everyone who searches finds,**
**and for everyone who knocks, the door will be opened.** *Luke 11:9–10*

Friends in Christ,
God knows our needs before we ask
and in our asking
prepares us to receive the gift of grace.

Let us open our lives to God's healing presence
and forsake all that separates us
from God and neighbor.

Let us be mindful not only of personal evil
but also of our communal sins
of family, class, race, and nation.

Let us confess to God whatever has wounded us
or brought injury to others,
that we may receive mercy
and become for each other
ministers of God's grace.

*Silence may be observed for examination of conscience.*

Let us confess our sins together.

**Merciful God,**
**we confess that we have sinned against you**
**in thought, word, and deed,**
**by what we have done,**
**and by what we have left undone.**

We have not loved you
with our whole heart and mind and strength;
we have not loved our neighbors as ourselves
In your mercy forgive what we have been,
help us amend what we are,
and direct what we shall be,
so that we may delight in your will
and walk in your ways,
to the glory of your holy name. Amen.

Or

Eternal God,
in whom we live and move and have our being,
your face is hidden from us by our sins,
and we forget your mercy in the blindness of our hearts.
Cleanse us from all our offenses
and deliver us from proud thoughts and vain desires.
In reverence and humility
may we draw near to you,
confessing our faults,
confiding in your grace,
and finding in you our refuge and our strength;
through Jesus Christ your Son. Amen.

*Assurance of God's forgiving grace is declared by the minister. These or other words may be used:*

The mercy of the Lord
is from everlasting to everlasting.
I declare to you, in the name of Jesus Christ,
you (we) are forgiven.

May the God of mercy,
who forgives you (us) all your (our) sins,
strengthen you (us) in all goodness
and by the power of the Holy Spirit
keep you (us) in eternal life.

**Amen.**

*Or*

Hear the good news!
Who is in a position to condemn?
Only Christ,
and Christ died for us,
Christ rose for us,
Christ reigns in power for us,
Christ prays for us.                                    *Rom. 8:34*

Anyone who is in Christ
is a new creation.
The old life has gone;
a new life has begun.                                  *2 Cor. 5:17*

Friends, believe the gospel.
In Jesus Christ, we are forgiven.

**Thanks be to God.**

*A joyful response is sung or said.*

### SCRIPTURE READINGS

*Before the reading of the scripture lessons, a prayer for illumination
is said by the reader.*

*Appropriate lessons from the scripture are read.*

### SERMON

*A sermon follows.*

*A psalm, a hymn, or a spiritual song may be sung.*

*When this service follows one that included confession of sin, the reading of scripture, and a sermon, the service shall continue from page 86, as follows:*

## OFFERING OF OUR LIVES TO GOD

*The minister or the leader says:*

I appeal to you therefore,
brothers and sisters,
by the mercies of God,
to present your bodies as a living sacrifice,
holy and acceptable to God,
which is your spiritual worship. *Rom. 12:1*

*Here all those present may ponder in silence all that is happening in their lives and, with renewed commitment, offer themselves and their gifts for ministry to the service of Jesus Christ in the world.*

## INTERCESSION FOR HEALING

*One of the following, or a similar prayer of intercession, is said:*

God, our creator,
your will for us and for all your people
is health and salvation:

**have mercy on us.**

Jesus Christ, Son of God,
you came that we might have life
and have it in abundance:

**have mercy on us.**

Holy Spirit,
your dwelling within us
makes us the temples of your presence:

**have mercy on us.**

To the triune God,
the source of all love and all life,
let us offer our prayers.

For all who are in need of healing,

   *Silence*

Lord, in your mercy,

**hear our prayer.**

For all who are disabled by injury or illness,

   *Silence*

Lord, in your mercy,

**hear our prayer.**

For all who are troubled by confusion or pain,

   *Silence*

Lord, in your mercy,

**hear our prayer.**

For all whose increasing years bring weariness,

   *Silence*

Lord, in your mercy,

**hear our prayer.**

For all about to undergo surgery,

   *Silence*

Lord, in your mercy,

**hear our prayer.**

For all who cannot sleep,

   *Silence*

Lord, in your mercy,

**hear our prayer.**

For all who practice the healing arts,

*Silence*

Lord, in your mercy,

**hear our prayer.**

*Here petitions for specific needs may be offered by the people.*

Into your hands, O God,
we commend all for whom we pray,
trusting in your mercy;
through Jesus Christ our Lord.

**Amen.**

### LAYING ON OF HANDS AND ANOINTING WITH OIL

*Those desiring the laying on of hands [and anointing with oil] come forward and bow or kneel. Each may make her or his request known to the minister(s) and/or to the elder(s).*

*One of the following prayers, or a similar prayer, is then said:*

WHEN ALL ARE TO RECEIVE THE LAYING ON OF HANDS AND ANOINTING:

Gracious God, source of all healing,
in Jesus Christ you heal the sick
and mend the broken.
We bless you for this oil
pressed from the fruits of the earth,
given to us as a sign
of healing and forgiveness
and of the fullness of life you give.
By your Spirit,
come upon all who are anointed with this oil,

that they may receive your healing touch
and be made whole,
to the glory of Jesus Christ our Redeemer.

**Amen.**

WHEN ALL ARE TO RECEIVE THE LAYING ON OF HANDS
(WITHOUT ANOINTING):

Gracious God, source of all healing,
in Jesus Christ you heal the sick
and mend the broken.
By your Spirit,
come upon all who receive the laying on of hands,
that they may receive your healing touch
and be made whole,
to the glory of Jesus Christ our Redeemer.

**Amen.**

*Or*

Lord and giver of life,
as by your power
the apostles anointed the sick,
and healed them,
so come, Creator Spirit,
and heal those who now receive the laying on of hands.

**Amen.**

WHEN AMONG THOSE TO RECEIVE THE LAYING ON OF HANDS,
SOME ARE TO BE ANOINTED AND OTHERS ARE NOT:

Gracious God, source of all healing,
in Jesus Christ you heal the sick
and mend the broken.
We bless you for this oil
pressed from the fruits of the earth,
given to us as a sign
of healing and forgiveness
and of the fullness of life you give.

By your Spirit,
come upon all who receive this ministry of compassion,
that they may receive your healing touch
and be made whole,
to the glory of Jesus Christ our Redeemer.

**Amen.**

> *The Lord's Prayer may be said by all (unless the Lord's Supper is to follow).*

As our Savior Christ has taught us,
we now pray:

Or

| | |
|---|---|
| **Our Father in heaven,** | **Our Father, who art in heaven,** |
| **hallowed be your name,** | **hallowed be thy name,** |
| **your kingdom come,** | **thy kingdom come,** |
| **your will be done,** | **thy will be done,** |
| **on earth as in heaven.** | **on earth as it is in heaven.** |
| **Give us today our daily bread.** | **Give us this day our daily bread;** |
| **Forgive us our sins** | **and forgive us our debts,** |
| **as we forgive those who sin** | **as we forgive our debtors;** |
| **against us.** | **and lead us not into temptation,** |
| **Save us from the time of trial** | **but deliver us from evil.** |
| **and deliver us from evil.** | **For thine is the kingdom,** |
| **For the kingdom, the power,** | **and the power, and the glory,** |
| **and the glory are yours** | **forever.** |
| **now and for ever. Amen.** | **Amen.** |

### LAYING ON OF HANDS

> *The minister and/or the elders lay both hands on the head of each individual and, after a brief silence, say:*

_____, may the God of all mercy
forgive you your sins,
release you from suffering,
and restore you to wholeness and strength.

**Amen.**

*Or*

_____, may God deliver you from all evil,
preserve you in all goodness,
and bring you to everlasting life;
through Jesus Christ our Lord.

**Amen.**

*Or*

Spirit of the living God, present with us now,
enter you, _____, body, mind, and spirit,
and heal you of all that harms you.
In Jesus' name.

**Amen.**

*Or*

_____, may the Lord Christ grant you healing.

**Amen.**

### ANOINTING WITH OIL

*If the person is to be anointed also, the leader dips her/his thumb in the oil and makes the sign of the cross on the person's forehead, adding these words to the formula used at the laying on of hands:*

I anoint you with oil
in the name of the Father,
and of the Son,
and of the Holy Spirit.

*Or*

As you are anointed with this oil,
so may God grant you the anointing of the Holy Spirit.

*The following prayer, or a similar prayer, is said:*

Mighty God,
you rise with healing in your wings,
to scatter all enemies that assault us.

As we wait in hope for the coming of that day
when crying and pain shall be no more,
help us by your Holy Spirit
to receive your power into our lives
and to trust in your eternal love,
through Jesus Christ our Savior.

**Amen.**

*Those who have received the laying on of hands (and anointing) are
dismissed with these or similar words:*

Go in peace to love and serve the Lord.

*A hymn may be sung.*

*If the Lord's Supper is to follow, the table may be prepared during
the singing of the hymn. The service will proceed with the order for
Holy Communion, beginning with the invitation to the Lord's Supper
on page 76.*

### BLESSING

*A blessing, such as one of the following, is given.*

The Lord bless you and keep you.
The Lord be kind and gracious to you.
The Lord look upon you with favor
and give you peace.                                        *Num. 6:24–26*

**Amen.**

*Or*

May the God of hope
fill you with all joy and peace in believing,
so that you may abound in hope
by the power of the Holy Spirit.                          *Rom. 15:13*

**Amen.**

# HYMNS, PSALMS, AND SPIRITUAL SONGS FOR PASTORAL CARE

*The following hymns, psalms, and spiritual songs are related to pastoral concerns and are appropriate for use in a service for wholeness.*

HB *The Hymnbook*
WB *The Worshipbook*
PH *The Presbyterian Hymnal*

## Hymns and Spiritual Songs

|  | HB | WB | PH |
|---|---|---|---|
| Abide with Me | 64 | 278 | 543 |
| All Hail the Power of Jesus' Name! | 132 | 285, 286 | 142, 143 |
| All Praise to Thee, My God, This Night | 63 | 292 | 542 |
| Amazing Grace, How Sweet the Sound | 275 | 296 | 280 |
| At Even, When the Sun Was Set | 55 | — | — |
| Be Still, My Soul | 374 | — | — |
| Breathe on Me, Breath of God | 235 | — | 316 |
| By Gracious Powers | — | — | 342 |
| Call Jehovah Your Salvation | 123 | 322 | — |
| Cast Your Burden on the Lord | — | 323 | — |
| Come Down, O Love Divine | — | 334 | 313 |
| Come, Thou Fount of Every Blessing | 379 | 341 | 356 |
| Come, Ye Disconsolate | 373 | — | — |
| Day Is Done | — | — | 544 |

| | HB | WB | PH |
|---|---|---|---|
| Eternal Light, Shine in My Heart | — | — | 340 |
| Fill My Cup | — | — | 350 |
| From Every Stormy Wind That Blows | 419 | — | — |
| Give to the Winds Thy Fears | 364 | 377 | 286 |
| Glorious Things of Thee Are Spoken | 434 | 379 | 446 |
| God Himself Is with Us | 13 | 384 | — |
| God Moves in a Mysterious Way | 112 | 391 | — |
| God of Compassion, in Mercy Befriend Us | 122 | 392 | 261 |
| God of Our Life | 108 | 395 | 275 |
| Great Are Your Mercies, O My Maker | — | — | 352 |
| Great Is Thy Faithfulness | — | — | 276 |
| Guide Me, O Thou Great Jehovah | 339 | 409 | 281 |
| Guide My Feet | — | — | 354 |
| Here, O Our Lord, We See You Face to Face | 442 | 418 | 520 |
| Holy Ghost, Dispel Our Sadness | — | — | 317 |
| Holy Spirit, Truth Divine | 240 | 422 | 321 |
| Hope of the World | 291 | 423 | 360 |
| How Firm a Foundation | 369 | 425 | 361 |
| I Greet Thee, Who My Sure Redeemer Art | 144 | 625 | 457 |
| I Love the Lord, Who Heard My Cry | — | — | 362 |
| I Want Jesus to Walk with Me | — | — | 363 |
| If Thou but Trust in God to Guide Thee | 344 | 431 | 282 |
| Immortal Love, Forever Full | 229 | — | — |
| Jesus, Lover of My Soul | 216 | — | 303 |
| Jesus, Priceless Treasure | 414 | 442 | 365 |
| Jesus, Remember Me | — | — | 599 |
| Jesus, Saviour, Pilot Me | 336 | — | — |
| Joyful, Joyful, We Adore Thee | 21 | 446 | 464 |
| Just as I Am, Without One Plea | 272 | — | 370 |
| Live Into Hope | — | — | 332 |
| Lord Jesus, Think on Me | 270 | — | 301 |
| Love Divine, All Loves Excelling | 399 | 471 | 376 |
| Loving Spirit | — | — | 323 |
| O Christ, the Healer | — | — | 380 |
| O God, in a Mysterious Way | — | — | 270 |
| O God, What You Ordain Is Right | 366 | 633 | 284 |
| O Love That Wilt Not Let Me Go | 400 | 519 | 384 |

| | HB | WB | PH |
|---|---|---|---|
| O Savior, in This Quiet Place | — | — | 390 |
| Praise, My Soul, the King of Heaven | 31 | 551 | 478 |
| Precious Lord, Take My Hand | — | — | 404 |
| Savior, Like a Shepherd Lead Us | 380 | — | 387 |
| Spirit of God, Descend Upon My Heart | 236 | 575 | 326 |
| Spirit of the Living God | — | — | 322 |
| The Lone, Wild Bird | 540 | 591 | 320 |
| There Is a Balm in Gilead | — | 600 | 394 |
| There's a Wideness in God's Mercy | 110 | 601 | 298 |
| Thine Arm, O Lord, in Days of Old | 179 | — | — |
| We Walk by Faith and Not by Sight | — | — | 399 |
| What a Friend We Have in Jesus | 385 | — | 403 |

### Psalms

*Psalm*

| | HB | WB | PH |
|---|---|---|---|
| 22—All Ye That Fear God's Holy Name | 35 | — | — |
| 22—Lord, Why Have You Forsaken Me | — | — | 168 |
| 23—The King of Love My Shepherd Is | 106 | 590 | 171 |
| 23—The Lord's My Shepherd, All My Need | — | — | 175 |
| 23—The Lord's My Shepherd, I'll Not Want | 104 | 592, 593 | 170 |
| 23—My Shepherd Will Supply My Need | — | 477 | 172 |
| 27—God Is My Strong Salvation | 347 | 388 | 179 |
| 31—In You, Lord, I Have Put My Trust | — | — | 183 |
| 34—The Lord I Will at All Times Bless | 412 | — | — |
| 42—As Deer Long for the Streams | — | — | 189 |
| 42—As Pants the Hart for Cooling Streams | 322 | — | — |
| 46—God Is Our Refuge and Our Strength | 381 | — | 191 |
| 51—God, Be Merciful to Me | 282 | — | — |
| 51—Have Mercy On Us, Living Lord | — | — | 195 |
| 63—O God, You Are My God | — | — | 198 |
| 63—O Lord, Our God, Most Earnestly | 327 | 514 | — |
| 63—O Lord, You Are My God | — | — | 199 |
| 90—Lord, You Have Been Our Dwelling Place | 88 | — | 211 |
| 90—Our God, Our Help in Ages Past | 111 | 549 | 210 |
| 91—Call Jehovah Thy Salvation | 123 | 322 | — |
| 91—Within Your Shelter, Loving God | — | — | 212 |

## OUTLINE OF A SERVICE FOR WHOLENESS FOR USE WITH AN INDIVIDUAL

Opening Sentences
Prayer
Scripture Reading
Laying On of Hands and Anointing with Oil
    Thanksgiving and Invocation
    Laying On of Hands
    [Anointing with Oil]
    Prayer
Blessing


## OUTLINE OF A SERVICE FOR WHOLENESS WITH REPENTANCE AND FORGIVENESS FOR USE WITH AN INDIVIDUAL

Opening Sentences
Prayer
Invitation to Confession
Prayer of Confession
Declaration of Pardon
Sign of Peace
Scripture Reading
Laying On of Hands and Anointing with Oil
    Thanksgiving and Invocation
    Laying On of Hands
    [Anointing with Oil]
    Prayer
Blessing

# OUTLINE OF A SERVICE FOR WHOLENESS WITH THE LORD'S SUPPER FOR USE WITH AN INDIVIDUAL

Opening Sentences
Prayer
Scripture Reading
Sermon
Laying On of Hands and Anointing with Oil
    Thanksgiving and Invocation
    Laying On of Hands
    [Anointing with Oil]
    Prayer
Invitation to the Lord's Supper
Great Prayer of Thanksgiving
    concluding with the Lord's Prayer
Breaking of Bread
    with Words of Institution
Communion
Prayer After Communion
Blessing

# OUTLINE OF A SERVICE FOR WHOLENESS WITH REPENTANCE AND FORGIVENESS AND THE LORD'S SUPPER FOR USE WITH AN INDIVIDUAL

Opening Sentences
Prayer
Invitation to Confession
Prayer of Confession
Declaration of Pardon
Sign of Peace
Scripture Reading
Sermon
Laying On of Hands and Anointing with Oil
   Thanksgiving and Invocation
   Laying On of Hands
   [Anointing with Oil]
   Prayer
Invitation to the Lord's Supper
Great Prayer of Thanksgiving
   concluding with the Lord's Prayer
Breaking of Bread
   with Words of Institution
Communion
Prayer After Communion
Blessing

# SERVICE FOR WHOLENESS
# FOR USE WITH AN INDIVIDUAL

*This service is for use in a hospital, a home, or a nursing home with individuals who are unable to attend a corporate service of wholeness.*

*It may be used in relation to the Service of Repentance and Forgiveness (pp. 112–113) and/or the celebration of the Lord's Supper (pp. 76–80).*

OPENING SENTENCES

*The minister says these or other words from scripture:*

Our help is in the name of the LORD,

**who made heaven and earth.** *Ps. 124:8*

*And one of the following:*

Those who wait for the LORD
shall renew their strength,
they shall mount up with wings like eagles,
they shall run and not be weary,
they shall walk and not faint. *Isa. 40:31*

Or

Give praise to God the Almighty,
by whose great mercy
we have been born anew to a living hope
through the resurrection of Jesus Christ from the dead. *1 Peter 1:3*

PRAYER

*The following prayer, or a similar prayer, is said:*

Let us pray:
God of compassion,
you have given us Jesus Christ, the great physician,
who made the broken whole
and healed the sick.
Touch our wounds, relieve our hurts,
and restore us to wholeness of life,
through the same Jesus Christ our Lord.

**Amen.**

*When the Service of Repentance and Forgiveness (pp. 112–113) is desired, it may be included here.*

### SCRIPTURE READING

*An appropriate passage from scripture may be read and briefly interpreted.*

### LAYING ON OF HANDS AND ANOINTING WITH OIL

*One of the following prayers, or a similar prayer, is said:*

IN RELATION TO LAYING ON OF HANDS
(WITHOUT ANOINTING):

Gracious God, source of all healing,
in Jesus Christ you heal the sick
and mend the broken.
By your Spirit,
come upon _____, who now receives the laying on of hands,
that *she/he* may receive your healing touch
and be made whole,
to the glory of Jesus Christ our Redeemer.

**Amen.**

*Or*

Lord and giver of life,
as by your power
the apostles anointed the sick
and healed them,
so come, Creator Spirit,
and heal _____, who now receives the laying on of hands.

**Amen.**

IN RELATION TO LAYING ON OF HANDS WITH ANOINTING:

Gracious God, source of all healing,
in Jesus Christ you heal the sick
and mend the broken.
We bless you for this oil
pressed from the fruits of the earth,
given to us as a sign
of healing and forgiveness
and of the fullness of life you give.
By your Spirit,
come upon _____, who now receives the anointing with oil,
that *he/she* may receive your healing touch
and be made whole,
to the glory of Jesus Christ our Redeemer.

**Amen.**

### LAYING ON OF HANDS

*The minister, or an elder, lays both hands on the person's head and,
following a brief silence, says:*

_____, may the God of all mercy
forgive you your sins,
release you from suffering,
and restore you to wholeness and strength.

**Amen.**

*Or*

_____, may God deliver you from all evil,
preserve you in all goodness,
and bring you to everlasting life;
through Jesus Christ our Lord.

**Amen.**

*Or*

Spirit of the living God, present with us now,
enter you, _____, body, mind, and spirit,
and heal you of all that harms you.
In Jesus' name.

**Amen.**

*Or*

_____, may the Lord Christ grant you healing.

### ANOINTING WITH OIL

*If the person is to be anointed also, the minister dips her/his thumb
in the oil and makes the sign of the cross on the person's forehead,
adding these words to the formula used at the laying on of hands.*

I anoint you with oil
in the name of the Father,
and of the Son,
and of the Holy Spirit.

*Or*

As you are anointed with this oil,
so may God grant you the anointing of the Holy Spirit.

*The following prayer, or a similar prayer, is said:*

Let us pray.

Blessed are you, O Lord our God,
Ruler of all creation.
We praise you for the abundance of your blessings.
To those who ask, you give love;
to those who seek, you give faith;
to those who knock, you open the way of hope.
Help us to serve you
in the power of the Holy Spirit,
through Jesus Christ our Lord.

**Amen.**

*Or*

Mighty God,
you rise with healing in your wings,
to scatter all enemies that assault us.
As we wait in hope for the coming of that day
when crying and pain shall be no more,
help us by your Holy Spirit
to receive your power into our lives
and to trust in your eternal love,
through Jesus Christ our Savior.

**Amen.**

*If the Lord's Supper is to be celebrated, the service will proceed with the order for Holy Communion, beginning with the invitation to the Lord's Supper on page 76.*

### BLESSING

*A blessing, such as the following, is given.*

May the God of hope
fill you with all joy and peace in believing,
so that you may abound in hope
by the power of the Holy Spirit.                    *Rom. 15:13*

**Amen.**

# SERVICE OF REPENTANCE AND FORGIVENESS FOR USE WITH A PENITENT INDIVIDUAL

# OUTLINE OF SERVICE OF REPENTANCE AND FORGIVENESS FOR USE WITH A PENITENT INDIVIDUAL

Invitation to Confession
Prayer of Confession
Declaration of Pardon
Sign of Peace
Going Forth

# SERVICE OF REPENTANCE AND FORGIVENESS FOR USE WITH A PENITENT INDIVIDUAL

*A penitent person who seeks an unburdening of conscience may seek the counsel of a minister. After counsel, the minister may suggest concluding the session with the following:*

## INVITATION TO CONFESSION

If we confess our sins,
God who is faithful and just
will forgive us our sins
and cleanse us from all unrighteousness.                    *1 John 1:9*

God, be merciful to me, a sinner.

_____, join me in a prayer of confession.

## PRAYER OF CONFESSION

*The minister and the penitent together pray this, or a similar, prayer of confession:*

Merciful God,
we confess that we have sinned against you
in thought, word, and deed,
by what we have done,
and by what we have left undone.
We have not loved you
with our whole heart and mind and strength;
we have not loved our neighbors as ourselves.
In your mercy forgive what we have been,
help us amend what we are,
and direct what we shall be,
so that we may delight in your will
and walk in your ways,
to the glory of your holy name. Amen.

## DECLARATION OF PARDON

*The minister will declare the assurance of God's forgiveness and speak confidently of the peace of God, in these or similar words:*

The mercy of the Lord
is from everlasting to everlasting.
I declare to you, in the name of Jesus Christ,
you are forgiven.

May the God of mercy,
who forgives you all your sins,
strengthen you in all goodness
and by the power of the Holy Spirit
keep you in eternal life.

**Amen.**

## SIGN OF PEACE

The peace of God, which surpasses all understanding,
will guard your heart and your mind in Christ Jesus.        *Phil. 4:7*

**Amen.**

## GOING FORTH

*After sharing a sign of God's peace, the minister concludes:*

Go in peace,
to love and serve the Lord.

# REAFFIRMATION OF
# BAPTISMAL VOWS
# FOR THE SICK OR THE DYING

# OUTLINE OF REAFFIRMATION OF BAPTISMAL VOWS FOR THE SICK OR THE DYING

Invitation to Reaffirmation of Baptismal Vows
Renunciation and Affirmation
Blessing [and Anointing]
Prayer
Sign of Peace
[Celebration of Holy Communion]

# REAFFIRMATION OF BAPTISMAL VOWS
# FOR THE SICK OR THE DYING

*This ceremony may take place at the bedside of the sick or dying person. Normally the minister will be accompanied by one or more elders.*

*The ceremony may also be used in the Service for Wholeness (pp. 104–108) for those who come together for the purpose of reaffirming their baptismal vows in the midst of illness.*

*One or more of the following scriptures may be read:*

*Psalm 23*                    *Luke 17:11–19*
*Psalm 46:1–5, 10–11*         *2 Corinthians 1:3–7*
*Psalm 90:1–10, 12*          *Philippians 4:4–7.*
*Psalm 91*

*Using these or similar words, the minister says:*

Through baptism you were joined to Christ,
in his death and resurrection,
and entered the covenant God has established.
In this covenant, the grace of God sustains and nourishes us
and strengthens our faith in the gift of life eternal,
which is ours in Christ.
Christ himself is our comfort and hope in illness.
It is he who brings us to wholeness of life.

*The minister continues, having determined whether all or any portions of the following renunciations and affirmations are appropriate in the situation:*

I ask you, therefore, once again to reject sin,
to profess your faith in Christ Jesus,
and to confess the faith of the church,
the faith in which we are baptized.

Do you renounce evil, and its power in the world,
which defies God's righteousness and love?

**I renounce them.**

Do you renounce the ways of sin
that separate you from the love of God?

**I renounce them.**

Do you turn to Jesus Christ
and accept him as your Lord and Savior?

**I do.**

Do you intend to be Christ's faithful disciple,
obeying his word, and showing his love, to your life's end?

**I do.**

Let us pray.

> *The minister offers a prayer that is relevant to the particular person(s)
> being ministered to. It may include thanksgiving, petition, interces-
> sion, confession, and forgiveness.*

> *The minister, laying hands upon each person who is sick or dying,
> offers the following prayer. The sign of the cross may be marked on
> the forehead of each person being ministered to, using oil prepared for
> this purpose:*

Defend, O Lord, your servant _____
with your heavenly grace,
that *he/she* may continue yours forever,
and daily increase in your Holy Spirit more and more,
until *he/she* comes to your everlasting kingdom.

**Amen.**

> *After each person has received the laying on of hands, the minister
> prays this or another appropriate prayer:*

Ever-living God, guard your *servant(s)* _____ , _____
with your protecting hand
and let your Holy Spirit be with *them* forever.
Lead *them* to know and obey your Word
that *they* may serve you in this life
and dwell with you in the life to come;
through Jesus Christ our Lord.

**Amen.**

The peace of Christ be with you.

**Amen.**

> *Holy Communion may be celebrated.*

# MINISTRY AT THE
# TIME OF DEATH

# MINISTRY AT THE TIME OF DEATH

*When death is near, the minister should be notified so that the ministry of the church may come to the dying person and the family.*

*The minister greets those present, saying:*

The Lord be with you.

**And also with you.**

We do not live to ourselves,
and we do not die to ourselves.
If we live, we live to the Lord,
and if we die, we die to the Lord;
so then, whether we live or whether we die,
we are the Lord's.                                    *Rom. 14:7–8*

　　　*Or*

God is our refuge and strength,
a very present help in trouble.                       *Ps. 46:1*

　　　*Or*

Praise be to the God and Father of our Lord Jesus Christ,
the Father of mercies and God of all comfort,
who comforts us in all our sorrows,
so that we can comfort others in their sorrow,
with the consolation we have received from God.       *2 Cor. 1:3–4*

　　　*This or a similar prayer is said:*

Gracious God, look on _____ ,
whom you created in your image,
and claimed as your own through baptism.
Comfort *her/him* with the promise of life eternal,
made sure in the death and resurrection of your Son,
Jesus Christ our Lord.

**Amen.**

*The Lord's Prayer is said.*

*One of the following is said:*

Lord Jesus Christ,
deliver your servant _____ from all evil
and set *him/her* free from every bond,
that *he/she* may rest with all your saints
in the joy of your eternal home
forever and ever.

**Amen.**

Gracious God,
sustain with your presence our *sister/brother* _____ .
Help *her/him* now to trust your goodness
and claim your promise of life everlasting.
Cleanse *her/him* of all sin
and remove all burdens.
Grant *her/him* the sure joy of your salvation,
through Jesus Christ our Lord.

**Amen.**

Almighty God,
by your power Jesus Christ was raised from the dead.
Watch over our *brother/sister* _____ .
Give *him/her* a vision of that home within your love
where pain is gone and death shall be no more.
For *his/her* perishable nature has put on the imperishable,
and *his/her* mortal nature has put on immortality,
and death is swallowed up in victory,
through Jesus Christ the Lord of life.

**Amen.**

_____ , our *sister/brother* in the faith,
we entrust you to God who created you.
May you return to the one who formed us out of the dust of the earth.
Surrounded by the great cloud of witnesses beyond all time and space,
may Christ come to meet you
as you go forth from this life.

May Christ, the Lord of glory,
who was crucified for you,
bring you freedom and peace.

May Christ, the High Priest,
who has forgiven all your sins,
keep you among his people.

May Christ, the Son of God,
who died for you,
show you the glories of his eternal kingdom.

May Christ, the Good Shepherd,
enfold you with his tender care.
May you see your Redeemer face-to-face
and enjoy the sight of God forever.

**Amen.**

*The minister lays his or her hand on the head of the dying person and says:*

Depart, O Christian soul, in peace;
in the name of God the Creator who formed you;
in the name of Jesus Christ who redeemed you;
in the name of the Holy Spirit the Comforter who sanctifies you.
In communion with the saints and all the heavenly host,
may you rest in peace,
and dwell forever with the Lord.

**Amen.**

*And*

Into your hands, O merciful Savior,
we commend your servant _____ .
Acknowledge, we humbly beseech you,
a sheep of your own fold,
a lamb of your own flock,
a sinner of your own redeeming.
Receive *him/her* into the arms of your mercy,
into the blessed rest of everlasting peace,
and into the glorious company of the saints in light.

**Amen.**

*The following prayer is said:*

O Lord, support us all the day long
of this troubled life,
until the shadows lengthen
and the evening comes
and the busy world is hushed,
and the fever of life is over,
and our work is done.
Then, in your mercy,
grant us a safe lodging,
and a holy rest,
and peace at the last;
through Jesus Christ our Lord.

**Amen.**

> *Prayers may be said for the family and friends of the dying, such as one of the following. Those who are present may be invited to offer prayers.*

Almighty God, our creator and redeemer,
you are our comfort and strength.
You have given us our *sister/brother* _____
to know and to love in our pilgrimage on earth.
Uphold us now as we entrust *her/him*
to your boundless love and eternal care.
Assure us that not even death
can separate us from your infinite mercy.
Deal graciously with us in our anguish,
that we may truly know your sure consolation
and learn to live in confident hope of the resurrection;
through your Son, Jesus Christ our Lord.

**Amen.**

Lord God,
look kindly upon us in our sorrow
as this life is taken from us,
and gather our pain into your peace.
Be with us in our grieving
and overcome all our doubts.
Awaken our gratitude for your gifts of love and tenderness.
As we are able to receive them,
teach us the lessons of life that can be learned in death.
We pray through Christ our Lord.

**Amen.**

Lead, kindly Light,
our only hope in darkness.
Heal the wounds of sorrow
and renew our trust in your goodness.
Enable us to be grateful
for the ties that bind us to _____ .
Renew our strength each day
to seek your will
and lean upon your mercy.
Keep us ever in the communion of saints
and in the promise of life eternal,
through Christ our Lord.

**Amen.**

God of compassion,
in sorrow we receive from you
the comfort you alone can give.
Enable us to see that you are always working for our good.
You are our dwelling place, O God,
and underneath us are your everlasting arms.
Assure us of your love,
that we may be able to accept
what we cannot understand.
Help us to be aware
not only of the darkness of death
but also of the splendor of life eternal.
Enable us even now to face life with courage;
give us the grace and the strength to go on,
knowing that the great cloud of witnesses surrounds us.

Let the life of _____ still inspire us.
Comfort and uphold us,
until we share together the light of your glory
and the peace of your eternal presence;
through Jesus Christ our Lord.

**Amen.**

*A blessing, such as the following, is given:*

The Lord bless you and keep you.
The Lord be kind and gracious to you.
The Lord look upon you with favor
and give you peace.                    *Num. 6:24–26*

**Amen.**

# NOTES

1. This text is from a medieval sequence hymn.

2. Directory for Worship, *The Constitution of the Presbyterian Church (U.S.A.), Part II: Book of Order* (Louisville, KY: Office of the General Assembly of the Presbyterian Church (U.S.A.), 1989), W-6.1003.

3. Augustine, "Sermon on Psalm 137," in *Expositions on the Book of Psalms* (Oxford: Parker, 1857), p. 162. Quoted in Kenneth L. Vaux, *Health and Medicine in the Reformed Tradition* (New York: Crossroad Publishing Co., 1984).

4. *Disciplinary Decrees of the General Councils*, trans. H. J. Schroeder (St. Louis: B. Herder Book Co., 1937), pp. 160, 163.

5. The Second Helvetic Confession, *The Constitution of the Presbyterian Church (U.S.A.), Part I: Book of Confessions*, 5.095.

6. Ibid., 5.234.

7. "The Form of Church Prayers," in *Liturgies of the Western Church*, ed. and trans. by Bard Thompson (Cleveland: Collins-World, 1961), p. 200.

8. *Letters of John Calvin*, ed. Jules Bonnet, vol. II (Philadelphia: Presbyterian Board of Publication, 1858), pp. 221–222 (Letter CCXL, 29th April, 1549).

9. William D. Maxwell, *The Liturgical Portions of the Genevan Service Book: Used by John Knox While a Minister of the English Congregation of Marian Exiles at Geneva, 1556–1559* (London: Faith Press, 1931), pp. 160–161. Text altered to present-day spelling.

10. *Calvin: Institutes of the Christian Religion*, trans. Ford Lewis Battles, ed. John T. McNeill, in Library of Christian Classics (Philadelphia: Westminster Press, 1960), vol. 1, pp. 638–639 (3.4.12).

11. Oil used in anointing is traditionally the finest grade of olive oil, to which other aromatic oil (perfume) is added. If olive oil is not available, other oil from plants is used. A small cruet or bowl facilitates the use of the oil. Oil prepared for anointing, and vessels crafted for its use, may be secured from some church supply houses. The regional supply stores related to Augsburg Fortress Publishers (426 South Fifth Street, Box 1209, Minneapolis, MN 55440; telephone 1-800-328-4648) are a readily available source for aromatic oils and vessels for anointing. Exceptionally fine concentrated oils are

available from Maria G. Arctander, 6665 Valley View Boulevard, Las Vegas, NV 89118. Both balsam and a Bethlehem Chrism are available. Bethlehem Chrism is a special blend of oils from flowers, herbs, and spices gathered from around the world. The concentrated oil is mixed with a high-grade olive oil for anointing. The same oils may be ordered from Liturgy Training Publications, 1800 North Hermitage Ave., Chicago, IL 60622-1101.

12. Geoffrey J. Cuming, ed., *Hippolytus: A Text for Students with Introduction, Translation, Commentary and Notes*, Grove Liturgical Study No. 8 (Bramcote, Nottinghamshire: Grove Books, 1976), p. 11.

13. *Music from Taizé* (Les Presses de Taizé [France], 1982, 1983, 1984); published in the United States by G.I.A. Publications, 7404 S. Mason Ave., Chicago, IL 60638. Two volumes in English are available, as well as one in Spanish.

14. The service contained in this book on pp. 117–120 is taken from *Holy Baptism and Services for the Renewal of Baptism: The Worship of God*, Supplemental Liturgical Resource 2 (Philadelphia: Westminster Press, 1985).

15. This service is based on Ministry at the Time of Death, in *The Funeral: A Service of Witness to the Resurrection*, Supplemental Liturgical Resource 4 (Philadelphia: Westminster Press, 1986), pp. 11–17, and is included here for the sake of convenience.

# SOURCES OF THE LITURGICAL TEXTS

BCP  *The Book of Common Prayer.* Episcopal Church, U.S.A., 1977.
BCW  *The Book of Common Worship.* Presbyterian, U.S.A., 1946.
FWR  *The Funeral: A Service of Witness to the Resurrection* (Supplemental Liturgical Resource 4). Presbyterian, U.S.A., 1986.
HBR  *Holy Baptism and Services for the Renewal of Baptism* (Supplemental Liturgical Resource 2). Presbyterian, U.S.A., 1985.
ION  *The Iona Community Worship Book.* The Iona Community, 1988.
LBW  *Lutheran Book of Worship.* Lutheran, U.S.A., 1978.
OCC  *Occasional Services.* Lutheran, U.S.A., 1982.
OCF  *Order of Christian Funerals.* International Commission on English in the Liturgy (Roman Catholic), 1985.
SLD  *The Service for the Lord's Day* (Supplemental Liturgical Resource 1). Presbyterian, U.S.A., 1984.
UCA  *Uniting in Worship.* The Uniting Church in Australia, 1984.
UCC  *Book of Worship.* United Church of Christ, 1986.
WBK  *The Worshipbook—Services and Hymns.* Presbyterian, U.S.A., 1972.
WTL  *Worship the Lord.* Reformed Church in America, 1987.

All scripture quotations are from the NRSV except as here noted. The following quotations are altered:
Num. 6:24–26 (pp. 80, 96, 128) is based on TEV as well as NRSV; Ps. 27:5 (p. 41); 1 Cor. 11:23–26 (p. 79); 2 Cor. 1:3–4 (p. 123); 2 Cor. 1:4ab, 5 (pp. 43, 86).
1 Peter 1:3 (pp. 43, 86, 104) is RSV alt.
Deut. 33:27a (p. 41) is from RSV.
Rom. 8:34 (p. 89) and 2 Cor. 5:17 (p. 89) are from Phillips' translation.
Rev. 3:20 (pp. 43, 75) is based on RSV and NRSV.

Sources of liturgical texts are acknowledged as follows:
pp. 64–65—"By your power . . ." WBK, altered.
p. 66—"Merciful God, your healing power . . ." WBK, altered.

pp. 67–68—"Mighty God, in Jesus Christ . . ." WBK, altered.

p. 70—"God of compassion and love . . ." OCC.

p. 70—"Merciful God, you strengthen . . ." UCA.

pp. 75, 87–88, 112—"Merciful God, we confess . . ." BCW, SLD, using BCP revision.

pp. 76, 88, 113—"The mercy of the Lord . . ." SLD. Based on declarations of pardon contained in BCW (1906, 1932, 1946).

p. 76—"According to Luke . . ." WBK, altered.

pp. 77–78—The Great Prayer of Thanksgiving. The opening dialogue (p. 77) and the "Holy, holy, holy Lord . . ." (p. 77) are agreed ecumenical texts prepared by the English Language Liturgical Consultation (1988). The prayer itself is from SLD, altered.

pp. 78, 94—"Our Father in heaven . . ." is an agreed ecumenical text prepared by the English Language Liturgical Consultation (1988).

p. 79—"The Lord Jesus, on the night . . ." Based on the RSV text of 1 Cor. 11:23–26 and Luke 22:19–20.

p. 80—"We thank you, O God . . ." UCA, altered.

p. 87—"Friends in Christ . . ." UCC, altered.

p. 88—"Eternal God, in whom we live . . ." BCW (1906, 1932, 1946). Abbreviated by Henry van Dyke (1852–1933) for BCW. Revised.

p. 89—"Hear the good news!" WBK, altered.

pp. 90–92—"God, our creator . . ." Based on a litany in WTL.

p. 92—"Into your hands . . ." LBW, altered.

pp. 95, 107—"Spirit of the living God . . ." ION, from the Service of Prayer for Healing in use in the Iona Community, where this petition is said by everyone together. Altered only in the adding of the person's name.

pp. 94, 106—"_____, may the God of all mercy . . ." BCP, altered.

pp. 118–120—Reaffirmation of Baptismal Vows for the Sick or the Dying is taken from HBR.

p. 119—"Defend, O Lord . . ." Based on a prayer in BCW order for the baptism of adults. Dating from the 1552 Book of Common Prayer, it is an abbreviated form of a prayer accompanying the laying on of hands in various sixteenth-century German confirmation orders. It continues to be included in the BCP.

pp. 123–128—Ministry at the Time of Death is based on the service by the same title in FWR.

p. 123—"Gracious God, look on . . ." FWR, altered.

p. 124—"Lord Jesus Christ . . ." BCP, adapted.

p. 124—"Gracious God, sustain . . ." FWR, altered.

p. 124–125—"_____, our sister/brother in the faith . . ." OCF, altered from the Roman Catholic Rite for the Commendation of the Dying.

p. 125—"Depart, O Christian soul . . ." BCP, altered.

p. 125—"Into your hands . . ." BCP.

p. 126—"O Lord, support us . . ." BCW, WBK, altered; attributed to John Henry Newman (1801–1890).

p. 126—"Almighty God, our creator . . ." FWR, altered.

p. 127—"Lord God, look kindly . . ." FWR, altered.

p. 127—"Lead, kindly Light . . ." FWR, altered.

p. 127—"God of compassion . . ." Based on a prayer in UCA.

# FOR FURTHER READING

Baer, Louis Shattuck, M.D. *Let the Patient Decide: A Doctor's Advice to Older Persons*. Philadelphia: Westminster Press, 1978.
> A seasoned family doctor/medical school professor's "patient-centered" approach to the question: "What can I do when my time comes to favor dying of natural causes in as short a time as possible?" as opposed to medically staving off death only to ensure lifeless years in an extended care facility.

Biegert, John E. *Looking Up . . . While Lying Down*. New York: Pilgrim Press, 1978, 1979.
> A small booklet of prayers and scripture readings that may be left with hospital patients to help them share their feelings with God while undergoing the trauma of hospitalization.

Bonhoeffer, Dietrich. *Spiritual Care*. Translated by Jay C. Rochelle. Philadelphia: Fortress Press, 1982.
> The bleak days of Nazi Germany that gave rise to the Confessing Church also gave birth to a tiny seminary in which Dietrich Bonhoeffer incubated and hatched his own Christocentric theology as well as nascent pastors for the Confessing Church. *Spiritual Care* is a collection of lectures through which Bonhoeffer shared with his brood of seminarians timeless theological principles of pastoral care. He addresses a variety of pastoral matters, including visits with those who are ill, dying, in grief, and "indifferent" to the gospel, stressing the importance of the pastor as "curate" of souls. A readable collection of essays, *Spiritual Care* is as much practical handbook as brilliant theological discourse.

_____. *Life Together*. Translated by John W. Doberstein. New York: Harper & Brothers, 1954.

The great twentieth-century Christian martyr explores how "the pris-
oner, the sick person, the Christian in exile sees in the companionship
of a fellow Christian a physical sign of the gracious presence of the
triune God." Bonhoeffer speaks powerfully of the efficacy of the mutual
confession of Christians and of the ministry of listening "with the ears
of God that we may speak the Word of God."

Clebsch, William A., and Charles L. Jaekle. *Pastoral Care in Historical Perspec-
tive.* Englewood Cliffs, N.J.: Prentice-Hall, 1964.
A classic account of the ministry of pastoral care as it has evolved in and
with the church through the ages.

Fink, Peter E., ed. *Alternative Futures for Worship.* Vol. 4, Paul J. Roy et al.,
*Reconciliation.* Collegeville, Minn.: Liturgical Press, 1987.
Fourth in a series of volumes that consider the sacraments of the Roman
Catholic Church in the light of the human sciences, including proposed
alternative liturgies for study use. This volume on reconciliation includes
essays on the psychological dimensions of reconciliation, the reconciliation of groups, the history and theology of reconciliation, and a series
of rituals imaging the future shape of reconciliation rites.

————, ed. *Alternative Futures for Worship.* Vol. 7, Orlo Strunk et al., *Anointing
of the Sick.* Collegeville, Minn.: Liturgical Press, 1987.
This volume on healing rites (seventh in the series noted above) includes
essays on the impact of the human sciences on healing ministry, theological reflections on healing ministry, history of healing and anointing in
the church, and a series of rituals aimed at more effective use of current
Roman Catholic healing rites as well as pointing the direction toward
shaping future healing liturgies.

Gusmer, Charles W. *And You Visited Me: Sacramental Ministry to the Sick and
the Dying.* Rev. ed. Vol. 6 in *Studies in the Reformed Rites of the Catholic
Church.* New York: Pueblo Publishing Co., 1989.
A careful overview of the history, meaning, and practice of rites attending ministry with the sick and with the dying within the Roman Catholic
tradition, with particular focus on the significant changes occurring since
Vatican II.

Holifield, E. Brooks. *A History of Pastoral Care in America: From Salvation to
Self-Realization.* Nashville: Abingdon Press, 1983.
A "case study" in itself, this volume traces the ways in which pastoral
care in America has reflected prevailing cultural ideas about human
nature at least as much as it has reflected denominational or doctrinal
distinctives.

Julian of Norwich. *Showings.* Translated by Edmund Colledge and James
Walsh. New York: Paulist Press, 1978.

A monument of the Western spiritual tradition relating a series of healing visionary encounters with the risen Christ, who assures Julian: "If I could love thee more, I would love thee more."

Kelsey, Morton T. *Healing and Christianity.* New York: Harper & Row, 1973.
This volume by a follower of Jung's psychology emphasizes the centrality of healing in the Christian gospel and the urge toward wholeness which is God's gracious gift in Christ: a gift revealed in the gospel, celebrated in liturgy, and to be appropriated in each human life.

McNeill, John T. *A History of the Cure of Souls.* New York: Harper & Brothers, 1951.
An encyclopedic history of the practice of ministry through the centuries, with particular emphasis on pastoral care.

Oden, Thomas C. *Pastoral Theology.* San Francisco: Harper & Row, 1983.
This work presents a systematic pastoral theology which explores and elucidates the self-understanding, role, and practice of the pastor. Oden sees all elements of ministry as an integrally related whole, rooted in the calling community, the church, and centered in the fact of Christ's ongoing ministry for and through us.

Ramshaw, Elaine. *Ritual and Pastoral Care.* Theology and Pastoral Care series. Philadelphia: Fortress Press, 1987.
Affirming the critical power of liturgical memory in the face of human need in both clinic and community, the author demonstrates how well performed and sensitively defined liturgy provides human vulnerability and sickness with not only an important memory but a re-presentation which elicits memories of the past and generates a hopeful present and future. Her section on Rites of Healing in the context of Ritual Care for the Individual reinvigorates the use of ritual and liturgy in a number of settings. A helpful attempt to explore the pastoral care dimensions of liturgy.

*Reformed Liturgy and Music,* vol. 24, no. 3 (Summer 1990). Theme: Pastoral Care (published in relation to the present volume, *Services for Occasions of Pastoral Care*).
This issue features articles on the theology that informs pastoral care, laying on of hands and anointing, ministry with the penitent, services for wholeness, changing role of hospital chaplaincy, pastoral care as part of health care team, the healing power of the use of hymns and psalms in ministry with the sick and the dying.

Vaux, Kenneth L. *Health and Medicine in the Reformed Tradition.* New York: Crossroad Publishing Co., 1984.
Considers major themes of theology and medicine in the light of the Reformed tradition. Themes include sexuality, birth, caring, pain, suffering, dying, health, and well-being. Reviews official church documents as well as the thought of leading Reformed theologians.

———. *This Mortal Coil: The Meaning of Health and Disease.* New York: Harper & Row, 1978.
An interpretation of the meaning of health and disease in the light of the scientific traditions of the West and the spiritual traditions of Judeo-Christianity.

Williams, Daniel Day. *The Minister and the Care of Souls.* New York: Harper & Row, 1961.
This work presents a theology of pastoral care, insisting that valid ministry is both grounded in and revelatory of the grace of God. Especially valuable is Williams's treatment of the dynamics of acceptance and forgiveness and their healing effect.

Winter, R. Milton. "Presbyterians and Prayers for the Sick: Changing Patterns of Pastoral Ministry," *American Presbyterians,* vol. 64, no. 3 (Fall 1986).
A historical survey of the way Presbyterians have sought to minister liturgically with the sick and the dying. Drawing upon service books and directories for worship, Winter shows the interplay between form and freedom characteristic of the Reformed tradition. Pastoral care at the time of the Reformation, and subsequently in Puritan England and in Scotland, and then in America are all considered.

The Order of St. Luke the Physician is comprised of clergy and laity within the church universal who feel impelled to make the ministry of healing a regular part of their vocation. *Christian Healing,* a handbook for members, is available from St. Luke's Press, P. O. Box 13701, San Antonio, TX 78213.

# ACKNOWLEDGMENTS

Material from the following sources is gratefully acknowledged and is used by permission. Adaptations are by permission of copyright holders. Every effort has been made to determine the ownership of all texts used in this resource and to make proper arrangements for their use. The publisher regrets any oversight that may have occurred and will gladly make proper acknowledgment in future printings if brought to the publisher's attention.

Scripture quotations from the Revised Standard Version of the Bible are copyrighted 1946, 1952, © 1971, 1973 by the Division of Christian Education of the National Council of the Churches of Christ in the U.S.A. and are used by permission.

Scripture quotations from the New Revised Standard Version of the Bible are copyrighted © 1990 by the Division of Christian Education of the National Council of the Churches of Christ in the U.S.A. and are used by permission.

Scripture quotations from *The New Testament in Modern English*, Revised Edition, translated by J. B. Phillips, are copyright © J. B. Phillips, 1958, 1960, 1972. Used by permission of Macmillan Publishing Company.

Scripture quotation marked TEV is from the *Good News Bible*, Today's English Version–New Testament, copyright © American Bible Society 1966, 1971, 1976.

*The Book of Common Worship*, copyright © 1932 and 1946 by The Board of Christian Education of the Presbyterian Church in the United States of America. Used by permission of Westminster/John Knox Press.

*Book of Worship*, © 1986 by permission of the United Church of Christ Office for Church Life and Leadership.

The English translation of texts prepared by the English Language Liturgical Consultation (ELLC), 1988.